a teacher's guide to
WRITING WORKSHOP
ESSENTIALS

Katherine Bomer AND Corinne Arens

a teacher's guide to

WRITING
WORKSHOP

ESSENTIALS

Time, Choice, Response

GRADES K–5

series editor Katie Wood Ray   **Heinemann** Portsmouth, NH

Heinemann

361 Hanover Street

Portsmouth, NH 03801–3912

www.heinemann.com

Offices and agents throughout the world

The authors and publisher wish to thank those who have generously given permission to reprint borrowed material:

Interior photographs: page 6, © Caia Images / Cavan Images; page 17, © Ian Allenden / Alamy Stock Photo; page 33,© WavebreakmediaMicro / Adobe Stock; page 54, © Aflo Co., Ltd. / Alamy Stock Photo; page 85, © Monkey Business Images / Shutterstock; page 99, © Gpointstudio / Adobe Stock; page 115, © Fuse / Jupiterimages/ Getty Images / HIP; page 117, © Diego Cervo / Adobe Stock; paint splatters used throughout, © ArtLana / iStock / Getty Images / HIP

Tweet by Ralph Fletcher. Copyright © 2018 by Ralph Fletcher. Reprinted with permission.

Library of Congress Cataloging-in-Publication Data

Names: Bomer, Katherine, author. | Arens, Corinne, author.

Title: A teacher's guide to writing workshop essentials : time, choice, response / Katherine Bomer and Corinne Arens.

Description: Portsmouth, NH : Heinemann, [2020] | Includes bibliographical references.

Identifiers: LCCN 2019045793 | ISBN 9780325099729

Subjects: LCSH: English language—Composition and exercises—Study and teaching (Elementary) | English language—Study and teaching (Elementary) | Writers' workshops.

Classification: LCC LB1576 .B5155 2020 | DDC 372.87/4—dc23

LC record available at https://lccn.loc.gov/2019045793

Editor: Katie Wood Ray

Production: Sean Moreau

Additional photography and videography: Sherry Day, Michael Grover, and Corinne Arens

Cover and interior designs, typesetting: Vita Lane

Manufacturing: Steve Bernier

Printed in the United States of America on acid-free paper

1   2   3   4   5   6   7   8   9   10   CGB   25   24   23   22   21   20

February 2020 Printing

We dedicate this book to Lucy Calkins and Donald Graves, who watched children write, listened to them talk about their process, and from that brilliant research, reimagined the way writing is taught in schools around the world.

Book Map

to begin

Writing Workshop Essentials 1

part 1

Time 7

part 2

Choice 35

About the Online Resources in This Book

In the online resources for this book, we've included a variety of forms and documents to use as you support your students with time, choice, and response in the writing workshop. You will find:

Supporting Young Writers at Home

Writing in Notebooks

Conferring at a Glance

Formative Assessment Form

Sample Conferring Forms

Different Kinds of Responses

Getting What You Need as a Writer

What to Do with Response

Supporting Appreciative Response

Reflecting on Work over Time

Look for this arrow throughout the book for resources that can be downloaded. See page x for instructions to access the online resources.

In addition to these resources, you will also find fifteen video clips highlighting time, choice, and response in action in writing workshops across grade levels.

VIDEO TITLE	VIDEO CONTENT	VIDEO TITLE	VIDEO CONTENT
Independent Writing Time	This clip shows what it looks and sounds like when K–5 students and teachers are engaged during independent writing time.	**Teaching a Minilesson with Mentor Texts**	In this clip, Georgiana uses a student mentor text to teach writers in first grade and reflects on the importance of mentor texts to students' development as writers.
Prioritizing Time	Teachers reflect on the importance of time to the work and development of writers and how they protect time for workshop each day.	**Conference with Izzy**	In this conference with a first grader, Katherine shows why having an enthusiastic, delighted *tone* is an important tool for children learning to write.
Routines in Action	A writing workshop thrives on structure and routines, and this clip showcases routines in action across grade levels.	**Teaching from Your Own Writing**	Students need to see their teachers as fellow writers, and in this clip, teachers in different grades use their own writing to teach a skill or strategy in minilessons.
Conference with Jeremiah	In this clip, Katherine confers with Jeremiah, a third grader, who seems to be practicing math rather than writing, but really just needs appreciative eyes to see the strengths in what he is doing, name them as such, and teach him how to use them for his writing.	**The Value of Response**	This clip shows the power of peer response in partnerships and small groups as K–5 students and teachers reflect on their importance.
Conference with Jalen	Katherine talks writer to writer as she confers with Jalen, a fourth grader, who's having a little trouble getting started.	**A Student Teaches the Class**	During share time at the end of each writing workshop, students often teach each other what they learned in conferences, as Siena, a third grader, shows in this clip.
The Importance of Topic Choice	K–5 teachers and students talk about how important choosing what to write about is to their engagement in the process.	**Teaching into Small-Group Work**	The best teaching is responsive teaching, and in this clip, Adri teaches "into" what she sees and hears her fourth graders doing as they meet in small groups.
Writing in Notebooks	Teachers and students in grades 3–5 reflect on the role of notebooks in the process of writing.	**Jackson and Tate Talk About Coauthoring a Series**	This video shows, better than we can tell, how time, choice, and response create skilled, passionate writers.
Students Engaged with Materials	This clip shows students choosing and using materials and space in different ways across grade levels.		

How to Access Online Resources

To access the online resources for *A Teacher's Guide to Writing Workshop Essentials*:

1. Go to **http://hein.pub/WritingWorkshop-login**.

2. Log in with your username and password. If you do not already have an account with Heinemann, you will need to create an account.

3. On the Welcome page, choose **"Click here to register an Online Resource."**

4. Register your product by entering the code: **WRITEWORK** (be sure to read and check the acknowledgment box under the keycode).

5. Once you have registered your product, it will appear alphabetically in your account list of **My Online Resources**.

Note: When returning to Heinemann.com to access your previously registered products, simply log into your Heinemann account and click on **"View my registered Online Resources."**

Acknowledgments
Take a Bow!

We have so many people to thank and only a little space to do it in, so we hope our colleagues and cheerleaders felt our deepest gratitude throughout the writing, filming, and production of this book. We especially want to thank

Dr. Annette Seago, Deputy Superintendent of the Blue Springs School District, Missouri, for her support and enthusiasm for this project, but more importantly, for her belief in sustained, quality professional development for teachers, and the space she provides for them to think, write, and learn together.

The principals at Chapel Lakes, Daniel Young, and Thomas Ultican Elementaries for opening their hearts and doors to our film crew, for rearranging schedules, and for even agreeing to be filmed conferring! Literacy coaches and teachers, for allowing us to capture their vibrant writing workshops in action; and children, for the delightful, brave, and pensive writing that graces these pages.

Heinemann Publishing, for inviting us to write this book. Our intuitive video producer, Sherry Day, and her talented camera and sound crew for making the book come to life on video. Deepest gratitude to our honorary "coauthors": Vita Lane, for the gorgeous visual design, Sean Moreau for the masterful production management, and Katie Wood Ray, for being such a staggeringly wise and helpful editor and for keeping the purpose and audience for this book front and center.

Katherine also thanks Ellin Keene, for generously recommending her to work with teachers on writing in BSSD, where Ellin transformed reading work and teacher collaboration for a dozen years; Corinne, for being the brightest thought companion and the most enthusiastic and compatible coauthor imaginable; and Randy, for always reminding her of what is essential. The concepts in this book created a kind of romantic playlist when they met at Teachers College Reading and Writing Project, and they still believe in them and talk about them endlessly, almost thirty years later.

Corinne would like to give a special thanks to Katherine, who "believed her up" into the role of an author. She thanks her colleagues and fellow coaches, who have fueled her with their dedication to kids, as well as Matt Glover, Ellin Keene, and Debbie Miller for their mentorship, friendship, and encouragement in the work of all things literacy. She would also like to thank each member of her loving and supportive family, especially the pieces of her heart that make it whole: Jeremy, Jude Larison, and Calista Nicole.

Writing Workshop Essentials

To begin

When Randy and I (Katherine) first saw our new home, for me at least, it was near unconditional love. It was an older home that its owners, artistic people, had transformed. They had painted the walls lush, majestic colors I would never have imagined and had filled their home with a courageous combination of antiques, modern furniture, and abstract art, everything so elegant and fun, it looked like an art gallery. I could see myself in this house becoming perhaps a more tidy and productive person, with new creative pursuits (cello lessons, perhaps?), and I could not let go of this vision of who I might become.

And then came the building inspection. Issues ranged from the mundane ("plants against the house need to be cut back at least eighteen inches to avoid moisture and pests") to the serious ("sloping floors and cracks in the walls from foundation shifts"). While the inspector remained upbeat and complimentary, he did finally look us square in the eye and admit with a sigh, "*All the bigs need love.*" The bigs meant foundation, roof, electrical, and plumbing. All the artful beauty of this dream home could not assure that it wouldn't just sink, sustain water damage, or spark an electrical fire until the crucial bare bones and systems of the structure were attended to.

The same is true in teaching. Even though we might discover the pitch-perfect minilesson that reaches all the students and makes them finally understand when to use *there*, *their*, and *they're*; even though we might display beautifully designed anchor charts in our HGTV classrooms full of bright furniture and color-coded baskets of books, if we have not attended to the essential "bigs," we may only be painting a pretty facade and not building and maintaining the solid structure that our students need in order to learn to write. When it comes to teaching writing, *all the bigs need love*. And the three bigs, the essential learning conditions that support a writing workshop—**time**, **choice**, and **response**—are what this book is all about.

All writers, young and old, need these three conditions to thrive. Time, choice, and response are the basic necessities we provide our students every day in the classroom, the over-and-over elements that allow for composition, thinking, creativity, and problem solving. We have seen this learning environment support countless writers, so we believe most students would grow as writers if this is *all* we gave them, every day: a chunk of uninterrupted time to write, a choice of what to write about and how to write it, and some time to share what they have written with peers and other audiences.

TIME, CHOICE, **AND RESPONSE** **IN ACTION**

Response

Their friends can't wait for the next install-ment of these chapter books, and this keeps the authors constantly looking out for new story ideas from life around them and from the books they read. They are sharpening their humor writing by noticing their audi-ence's response—what they laugh at and which books are group favorites.

Choice

These young authors choose to make these stories about the antics of animal characters named after themselves and their friends. They choose to illustrate their stories or not, in black and white or color, and to fashion them into tiny stapled booklets so they fit into plastic sleeves from old game trading cards.

Time

Two young authors, Jackson and Tate, have been writing their chapter book series together for more than a year, reaching a total of more than 160 books. The more time they spend working on these books, the stronger their understandings of narrative structure, dialogue, humor, audience preferences, and revision become. And the more they learn to love to write.

Forest Fire
By TJ

Chapter 1
what happend
It all started with a bomfire. It forgot to get put out, and now the city is under atack! fire

fiters planers and even hoses have tride to put it out, but only one man can stop it!

I survived a weekend at gramma's hous
by Jack Carter

Chapter 1
the mesage
One day Bob Was about to get out of school. then the intercome came on. Bob your grandma Will pick you up today. Oh no Bob new what Was coming. a Weekend at grandma's house.

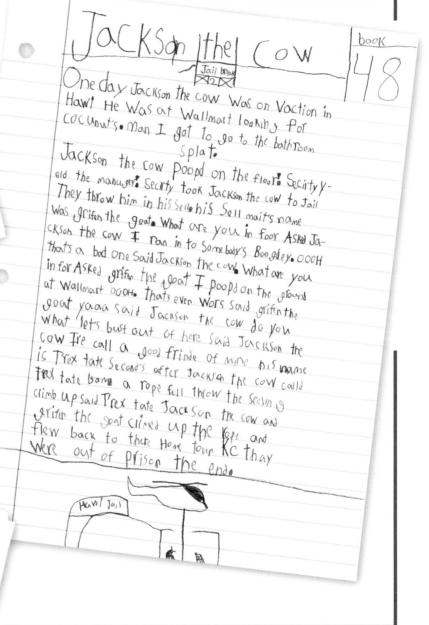

Jackson the cow   book 48

Jail break

One day Jackson the cow Was on Vaction in Hawi! He Was at Wallmart looking for cocunut's. Man I got to go to the bathroom splat.

Jackson the cow poopd on the floor! Secirty told the manuger! Secirty took Jackson the cow to Jail. They throw him in his Sell. his Sell mait's name Was grifen the goat. What are you in foor Asked Jackson the cow I ran in to Somebody's Boo gedey. OOOH that's a bad one Said Jackson the cow. What are you in for Asked grifen the goat I poopd on the ground at Wallmart OOOH. that's even Wors said grifen the goat yaaa said Jackson the cow do you what let's bust out of here said Jackson the cow I'e call a good frinde of mine his name is Trex tate Second's after Jackson the cow caild Trex tate bamm a rope fell throw the Seclin g climb up said Trex tate Jackson the cow and grifen the goat climed up the rope and flew back to there Home tour KC thay Were out of Prison the end.

Hawi Jail

We realize that an environment—an artful dream house—built on a foundation of time, choice, and response might be hard to visualize, especially if you're new to writing workshop. But even if you're experienced, it can be challenging to keep the workshop running day after day, so we offer this book full of words, images, and videos to help you imagine your own writing workshop and face the challenges.

We hope that many of the ideas for teaching writing in this book feel big to you, but not overwhelming. We hope that as you read, there are places where you breathe a sigh of relief when you recognize something familiar. Or maybe you will find something that you can, with a few tweaks, seamlessly add to the mix of your current writing instruction. We also hope that you discover ahas, little revelations, like how, for instance, students can have more choice in genre studies.

In the house you build from time, choice, and response, there also needs to be space for grace and truth. Grace will get you through the times of insecurity when you ask yourself if you even know what you are doing. Truth will help you align your actions and beliefs. It will help you determine if what you hope and desire *most* for writing instruction is happening within your classroom.

All the bigs need love, and we hope this book will give you confidence to embrace time, choice, and response as foundational conditions for learning how to write, and as the *what* and the *why* to all your most important teaching decisions.

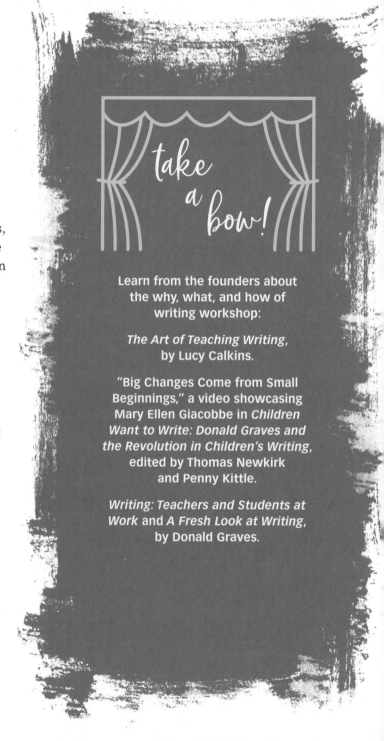

take a bow!

Learn from the founders about the why, what, and how of writing workshop:

The Art of Teaching Writing, by Lucy Calkins.

"Big Changes Come from Small Beginnings," a video showcasing Mary Ellen Giacobbe in *Children Want to Write: Donald Graves and the Revolution in Children's Writing*, edited by Thomas Newkirk and Penny Kittle.

Writing: Teachers and Students at Work and *A Fresh Look at Writing*, by Donald Graves.

Writing Workshop Structure

Lucy Calkins, Donald Graves, and Mary Ellen Giacobbe developed an elegant classroom structure to encompass the essentials for teaching and learning how to write. This simple structure has been practiced and refined for four decades, and it has become what writing instruction looks like every day in thousands of K–12 classrooms around the world.

MINILESSON

Students receive direct instruction from the teacher, a guest writer, or a student in some aspect of the writing process, kinds of writing, composition techniques, language skills, or materials and tools.

INDEPENDENT WRITING TIME

Students focus on their writing work and the teacher confers with individuals, partners, or small groups.

SHARE TIME

Students teach each other as they share something about their writing or their process with a partner, a small group, or the whole class.

The predictable workshop "architecture" of minilesson, independent writing time, and share allows creativity to explode because it moves writers into what Donald Graves (1994) called "a constant state of composition" (104). Students can *count* on having time to compose texts on paper or screen. If a writer runs out of time to finish their story today, no problem, they can come back to the work tomorrow—same time. If a writer gets an idea for their feature article while they're talking with a friend after school, no problem—they can write it in their notebook and work on it tomorrow—same time. Each day's minilesson lays another brick on the structure, and each time students write, revise, share, and give each other feedback, they add mortar. The classroom community is building a culture of writing together, and it takes time.

A Note on Direct Instruction

On any given day, the minilesson you see is probably just one in a whole series of lessons. Because there are very few things you can teach about writing in just one lesson, teachers almost always plan for a *series* of lessons—called a unit of study—that lasts anywhere from a week to three or four weeks.

The Power of Rituals and Routines

Think about how an art studio, religious service, and a baseball game have predictable, focused, purposeful structures. Once we experience these spaces, our mind and body know what to expect and we can relax into the experience—to create more, listen more actively, or play a better game—without worrying about what comes next. Similarly, we create rituals and routines in the writing workshop so students can focus on writing. The more time spent experiencing the predictable structure of the workshop, the more energy and mindfulness can be directed toward creating, composing, and sharing.

Time

**part
one**

How much time did it take for you to learn to read or ride a bike? How much time did it take to understand another language or to solve algebraic equations? How long did it take for Michelangelo to paint the Sistine Chapel or for the founders to agree upon and craft the Constitution of the United States of America? How many hours of intense dance and gymnastics training did it take for Simone Biles to perfect her superhuman floor routine flip, now named "The Biles"?

We know that everything lovely, difficult, necessary, and meaningful takes time. We do not question this.

Writing also takes time. Authors need time to craft their novels, articles, poems, and plays. Professionals need time to compose reports, ads, and websites. There is no way around the fact that writing takes time from initial idea, to draft(s), to revising and editing, to the final product. Time is the only absolute about the writing process—nothing gets written without it!

Young writers need time to write, but they also need time to learn how to write well. Our students must experience taking a piece of writing *through* time and practice how to manage themselves *in* time—how to breathe through frustration, sit through multiple rereadings, make changes, and solve sticky problems that arise in crafting sentences and paragraphs. The strategies we teach students for working through this process in time actually form the curriculum of writing. If students aren't spending *time* writing, they're not learning how to write.

Writers also need *uninterrupted* time. Schools are sometimes the most disruptive places to learn. Trying to write at school reminds us of trying to rest and heal in a hospital bed, when attendants come at all hours to check vitals, make us swallow big pills, and deliver something they call "food." Writing workshop doesn't need to feel like a hospital. We can create and protect an uncluttered, uninterrupted space for thinking, writing, and responding each day—a precious bubble of time that should not be pierced for any reason. Though there are stops and starts on each day's journey of pieces of writing, the work of writing isn't "over" until the clock says it's time for lunch or math. Once the workshop is a daily routine, kids will be upset if it doesn't occur. This time of day becomes an appointment you look forward to, like recess or lunch or soccer practice.

Supporting Young Writers at Home

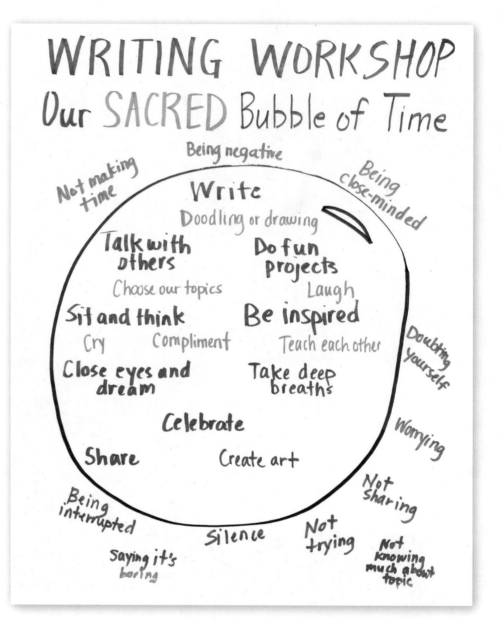

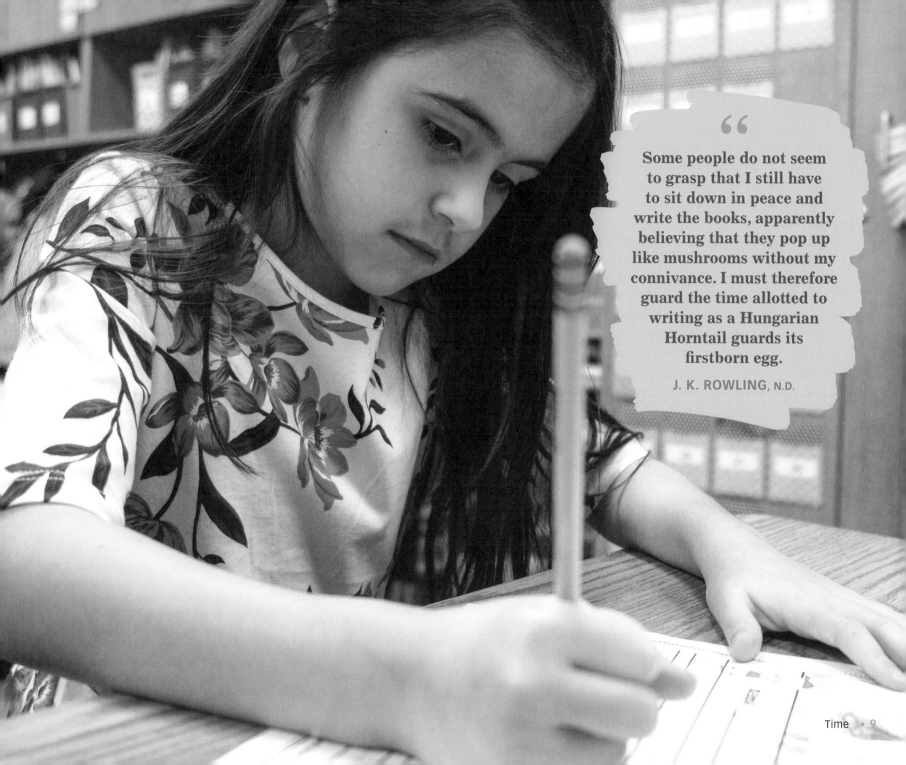

> Some people do not seem to grasp that I still have to sit down in peace and write the books, apparently believing that they pop up like mushrooms without my connivance. I must therefore guard the time allotted to writing as a Hungarian Horntail guards its firstborn egg.
>
> J. K. ROWLING, N.D.

Working in Time

Because writing workshop is a *time*, not a task like a prescribed activity or worksheet, no one races to finish so they can go and do something else—say, finish social studies homework or play a math game. In the writing workshop structure, after the minilesson, everyone in the room is attending to projects for the entire thirty to forty minutes of independent writing time. Students have work to do and decisions to make about whatever project they are working on. In many classrooms, students actually have *several* writing projects they are working on independently, and of course, students can always start a new piece at any time.

Types of Projects That Occur Across Time in the Writing Workshop

INDEPENDENT WRITING PROJECTS

Students have time to design, explore, and compose writing projects they have chosen. Perhaps they have been itching to write a letter to a friend who moved to another state, or to compose lyrics to a song that has been burning in their heart, or to practice a spoken word poem.

DIGITAL PROJECTS

Students have time to explore safe digital spaces for writing and for creating print and visual texts: digital storytelling, movie making, animations, or products from word processing templates like invitations, posters, flyers, or pamphlets.

COLLABORATIVE WRITING PROJECTS

Students work with a partner or two on dream projects: a play about unicorns, a fan-fiction piece for a website, a how-to book about the video game they play together after school.

WRITING PROJECTS CONNECTED TO A GENRE STUDY

At certain times of the year, the whole class may be studying a particular kind of writing for several weeks. During these studies, students are working on at least one writing project in that genre, about a topic they have chosen and through a process they determine.

1 Drafting a Book on Dinosaurs

2 Composing a Notebook Entry

3 Editing Prior to a Celebration

4 Studying a Mentor Text

What Students Do in the Writing "Bubble of Time"

Writing is a process that unfolds in different ways, and the process is always in motion, so it's hard to say when one "step" of it begins and another one ends. On any given day, different students might be engaged in a range of writing process activities that support their different projects.

If you glance at this graphic and think, "Yikes, that just looks chaotic," don't worry. Around the outside of the circle are the basic moves of the writing process. This is generally how a piece of writing travels through time, from idea generating and planning to drafting, revising, editing, and publishing. These basic moves give you a kind of structure in which to place all the writing actions you see inside the circle.

Reading mentor texts
- Deconstructing texts (poems, blogs, memoirs, essays) to learn how they are built.
- Naming organization and style decisions the author made.

Writing to think, remember, record, question
- In a writer's notebook . . .
- Exploring thoughts, feelings, wonderings, ideas, memories.
- Making lists and plans.
- Practicing writing. Trying things out.
- Sketching and drawing.

Idea generating
- Making lists. Freewriting.
- Talking through possibilities with partners.

Choosing a Topic
- Rereading notebooks and writing folders to look for possible topics.

Planning
- Making outlines, storyboards, webs, quick writes.

Drafting
- Trying out different ways a piece could go, different genres, style moves, dialogue.
- Writing more.
- Getting started.

Revising
- Elaborating.
- Trying new beginnings and endings.
- Rereading writing to look for places to cut, add, and change.

Editing
- Rereading for missing words, misspellings, punctuation.

Publishing
- Word processing, formatting, illustrating.

Thinking About Beginning Writers

Pictorial Support to Build Independence

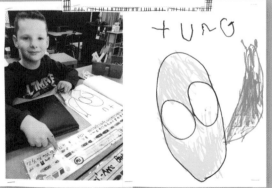

I can add letters and words to my book.

I can use tools around the room to help me.

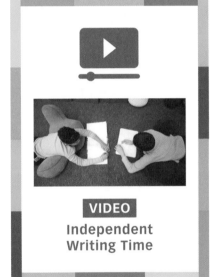

VIDEO

Independent Writing Time

If you have plenty of paper choices and writing tools available, beginning writers easily use the writing process to make all kinds of things: picture books, cards, signs and labels, poems, songs, letters. They don't write quickly, of course, so most of their thinking, idea generating, and planning will happen through talk (before, during, and even after!) instead of writing. If you want to see a kindergarten teacher get her students started in writing workshop on the very first day of school, check out another book in the Classroom Essentials series, *A Teacher's Guide to Getting Started with Beginning Writers*, by Katie Wood Ray and Lisa Cleaveland.

But What About...?

Don't I need to teach my students the steps of the writing process before I let them go in a writing workshop?

You don't! To put anything on paper, students have to use some kind of process. If your students have never been in a writing workshop before, just talk a little about the different kinds of things writers make and do—perhaps chart a few possibilities—then give them some writing tools and materials and let them get started. You will quickly see what they do and don't yet know, and you will get all kinds of ideas for the teaching they need. And remember, you've got a whole year's worth of teaching to support them in getting better at every aspect of the writing process.

TIME, CHOICE, **AND** RESPONSE **IN ACTION**

Response

Though his written text is not yet conventional, his teacher and friends know the book says, "Go mermaid! Go mermaid! Go mermaid!" because that's how he read it several times aloud.

Choice

Ellison loves mermaids, and he loves writing workshop because he gets to write about mermaids every day if he wants to.

Time

Ellison worked on his "Go, Mermaid!" book over several days, and it shows in the careful details of the mermaids' bodies, hair, faces, the pirate ship, and the segmented colors. He added speech bubbles like he has seen in mentor picture books.

What Teachers Do in the Writing "Bubble of Time"

In writing workshop, we write and learn alongside our students, and they come to see us as fellow writers. We teach something about writing in a short lesson, with our students gathered close to learn and reflect with each other. When we demonstrate something from our own writing, we demystify the process, break it into digestible and doable bits, so that our students can try those out, following our example, and then begin to develop a process of their own.

When students settle into their spots to write, we put ourselves right in the middle of their work. In writing conferences, we sit next to individual writers and teach in response to their needs. Sometimes, if we see that several students need the same writing lesson, we gather them in a small group and offer the teaching they need.

When there are only five to ten minutes left, we might ask students to turn to a partner and take turns sharing something they wrote or learned how to do, or need help with. Or we might signal for students to come back together as a whole group and ask a few of them who discovered something or tried a new strategy to teach the class about it. At this moment, we step back from the teacher role and we become "writer-whisperers," helping students who are sharing to speak loudly, show their work, and ask for responses from the rest of the class.

Teach and demonstrate aspects of writing.

Write alongside students occasionally.

Confer one-on-one with students or with partnerships and small groups of students who need the same teaching point.

Research students' writing to inform instruction.

> **"** Children learn to control writing because their teachers practice teaching as a craft. Both teachers and children see the control of the craft as a long, painstaking process with energy supplied along the way through the joy of discovery.
>
> DONALD GRAVES, 1983B, 3

Predictable Time Matters

Ideally, you'll want to plan for your writing workshop to happen at the same time every day for forty-five to sixty minutes. When you make writing time predictable, there are many benefits.

Instructional Benefits

- Protecting a block of time sends a clear message that writing is important and deserves daily attention.

- A protected writing block gives kids space to tune into their own thinking, solve writing problems, and make decisions.

- Students have more time to reread their work, which leads to revising and editing, which teaches that writing can always get better.

- Creating space in the schedule to talk about writing with others helps kids get ideas and important feedback for revising and editing.

- Establishing expectations for movement, noise levels, and activity saves precious minutes for writing.

- Students have more time to take charge of managing their own plans, processes, and products.

Social-emotional Benefits

- Time to think is a gift that can help kids relax and stay calm in a busy or stressful school schedule.

- Kids learn that thinking and writing evolves, slowly and surely, across stretches of time—they do not have to have the "right answer" instantly.

- Writers have chances to change their minds and to both make and fix mistakes.

- Children grow in spurts and at different times—they do not all master a concept at the same time.

- Students learning English as an additional language benefit from having more time to practice writing and gain confidence.

We want it to have that accepted, routine, sunrise-sunset kind of dependability in students' understanding of how the day goes. Writing workshops break down when they lose this quality, when they become questionable, when the teacher may decide, 'We're not having it today.'

KATIE WOOD RAY, 2001, 52

But What About ...?

What if it's just not possible for me to have writing workshop at the same time every day?

You don't have to give up because of this obstacle. What matters most is that the rituals and routines *inside* the bubble of time are consistent and predictable, and that students know they can count on having workshop time every day. If that time has to be a little later one day than another, it breaks the rhythm of the day slightly, but you'll still reap the same benefits over time as students become accustomed to the schedule.

Work That Extends *Across* Time

Students who are new to writing workshop may have experienced only task-like schoolwork that they finished quickly, and the idea of working on the same thing across days of time will be new. So, in addition to helping them imagine all the moves they can do *in* time, you can also help them think about their work *across* time:

- In conferences, ask individual students how they plan to continue working on their writing tomorrow.

- At the end of share time, invite students to think about what they will be doing tomorrow. You can say, "Make a plan for writing while today's work is still fresh in your mind." They can hold this plan in their thinking or write it in their notebooks or on a sticky note to keep in their folders.

- In minilessons, demonstrate how writers reread their work at the beginning of each day's new work, going back in time to capture their momentum before moving forward with new writing.

A student has time to work and space to spread out multiple drafts.

- Highlight what it means to stay with a project—the kind of power that comes with endurance—and let children talk about what they are doing to stay with a piece of writing over time.

Protecting Writing Workshop Time

Sometimes as teachers, we're tempted to think, "I simply don't have enough time for a writing workshop or to let students gradually evolve as writers."

But it's not really that we don't have time. In most elementary schools, we have anywhere from five to seven instructional hours a day, for at least 180 days. The question is, How do we use the time we have? Do we fill the time devoted to writing with isolated skills instruction and worksheets for punctuation, handwriting, and vocabulary? Or do we, instead, guard that time to teach kids how to write to think; how to compose essays, stories, and informational texts; how to revise and edit their writing to make it appealing for readers; and how to share it with others? We believe the second possibility for using time provides enticing, purposeful places to teach punctuation, handwriting, and vocabulary in ways that stick. And we believe that learning to write broadly, deeply, and well has benefits beyond the classroom and for the rest of students' lives.

To accomplish this, we have to be proactive about protecting the time we set aside for writing. There are so many things pulling at us and at our schedules; these may be wonderful, even necessary things, like fire drills or a performance from a local dance troupe, but we have no say about them. We *do*, however, have control over other activities—it's just a matter of deciding what matters most and then prioritizing.

Let's think for a moment about activities in a typical school day that can take up more time than they might need. As you look at these time stealers, ask questions like "Can I tuck this teaching easily into the writing workshop?" "Can I tighten this transition up a bit?" and "Do I really need this?"

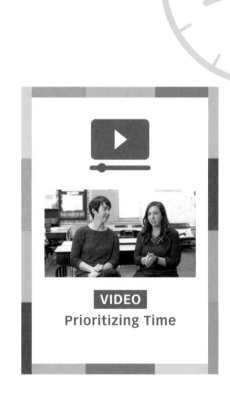

VIDEO
Prioritizing Time

Time Stealers

- Transitions—in the writing workshop and all day long

- Isolated skills practice

- Yearlong test preparation and practice

- Extracurricular clutter (holiday craft projects)

- Mastery expectations (waiting until every student "gets" each concept or skill before moving along)

- Assumptive teaching—teaching things many kids may not need

Time Savers

Luckily, most of these time stealers can be turned into time savers, and there are lots of practical ways you can free up time both inside and outside the writing workshop. Adopting time savers like these will give you confidence in your schedule and help you say, "I *do* have time for writing workshop!"

Establish and Practice Routines

Decide how your students will move through the classroom safely, and then teach them: from minilesson area to work areas and back; from

Chart with Pictures of Students Practicing Workshop Routines

work areas to a writing station to get more supplies or to the classroom library to get a mentor text to put next to their writing. Teach kids how to turn quickly and without argument to a writing partner or just the person sitting next to them during the minilesson. Teach them how to clean up after writing, where to replace materials, and where to put their writing notebooks, drafts, and writing folders. Practice these movements right from the start of the school year, and with students' input, solve any issues that arise, then follow up and fine-tune as you go.

Create a Predictable, Consistent Start and End Time

 Whether you choose 9:00 a.m. or 2:30 p.m., try to protect the time you choose for writing workshop as much as you are required to honor the lunch and specials schedule. Your students will quickly come to see the workshop as a daily routine, and they will come "ready to write" with whatever materials they need for the minilesson and with ideas, questions, and a need to learn what you are teaching.

Invite Students to Help You

Transfer of responsibility is another way to think about saving time. Ask yourself, "What do I do that students could be doing independently with a process or structure that works and some practice?" Consider tasks like

- passing out supplies

- using tricky supplies, such as a pencil sharpener, stapler, or tape dispenser

- getting additional supplies as needed—paper, writing utensils, tape, and scissors—without asking for permission

- answering questions and offering suggestions (turning to a partner or small writing group for help)

VIDEO
Routines in Action

Teach Students to Be Problem Solvers

Don't let students line up behind you with questions, as this turns you into a problem solver and an editor rather than a teacher. It wastes their time and yours. Instead, empower kids with strategies for reading their own work and self-editing, or turning to writing partners for feedback. Also, provide clear expectations for what kids should do when they feel "finished" with their writing. As a reminder, consider posting an ongoing anchor chart with a list of writing-centered tasks for students to reference as possibilities. You might also bring the question "What do writers do when they feel stuck or finished?" to share time and chart the answers of fellow writers in the classroom.

Consider Different Scheduling Options

Find required (or desired) activities in your schedule that can be tucked into other structures and routines. For example, you might move handwriting practice to a learning station, practice spelling words and punctuating sentences during morning work, or carve out a ten-minute word study each day. Put holiday-themed activities and projects into a learning station or a "choice time" on a single Friday afternoon.

I'm finished...
what can I do??

- re-read my piece
- work on my independent writing project
- get with a writing partner
- revisit my notebook
- start a new piece
- sketch into a new idea
- check out mentor text

Teach Writing Skills as Needed in Minilessons and Conferences

The mechanical features of written language matter tremendously—but only if students are composing real texts so they experience their true value. If you teach grammar and punctuation as a sort of "secret code" that allows readers to read students' spooky stories or their passionate pleas to ban plastic bags, kids tend to be more interested in using them as tools to enhance their writing. When lots of students are editing and getting ready to publish their work, you can teach how to use commas to set off a parenthetical phrase, for instance, in a minilesson where students can turn their full attention to the surface features of language. Then follow through by helping students apply these features to their individual pieces during writing conferences.

Plan Ahead for Predictable Teaching

Trying out different strategies for writing and talking about your decisions in front of students creates a powerful demonstration of whatever you want to teach (and it teaches you so much about writing as well), but it takes time. To save time, plan ahead for this teaching: write in your own writing notebook, and make poems, stories, picture books, and essays along with your students to use as demonstration texts. Keep your drafts and finished writing, artifacts, and reflections from each year to use as mentor texts for your current class.

  Another way to plan ahead for predictable teaching and save time is to preview student work prior to conferring—do this after school or take a quick look in the morning (for just those four or five students you are going to confer with that day).

See Learning to Write as an Evolution Rather Than "Mastery"

When you come to trust that how people learn to do anything well is through practice, through fits and starts, and through failures and mini-successes, you will experience time expanding rather than feeling a lack of time. On the other hand, if you stop the presses because six children still produce solid blocks of text, though you have taught how to indent paragraphs fifteen times, you lose valuable practice time for everyone. Instead, try addressing an issue like this in individual conferences or small groups with children who need more support. Or you can trust that writing is a recursive practice, that their learning will evolve over time, and that the paragraphing light bulb might suddenly appear three months later, or that it might make more sense when they're writing a short story than a persuasive essay. To build trust in students' learning over time, consider saving student work and date-stamping each piece—the growth will be obvious!

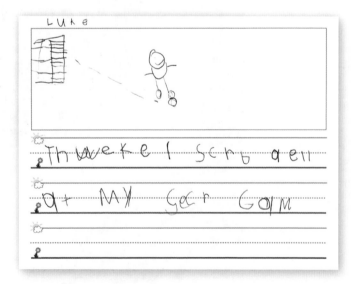

A student writes about soccer in kindergarten . . .

. . . and again in third grade. Look at his growth!

But What About...?

What if I have a student who feels afraid to write? And what if all that time for writing feels like too much time?

Good question! Here are several possibilities:

- Offer the child doable goals with questions like these:

  - ➜ How far down this one piece of paper could you write? Show me. Put a little mark there and go for it!

  - ➜ How many pages of your [three- to five-page] book do you think you can you fill about that?

  - ➜ How about we set this timer and see how much you can write for ten minutes?

  - ➜ Could you draw/sketch yourself into something to write about?

- Build a theory through conversations and observations about what might be causing the child some anxiety. Often, the fear is about doing something "wrong," so be sure to create an appreciative, accepting environment.

- Demonstrate most often with your own unfinished, imperfect drafts, not with edited, polished writing.

Assess Often to Know What to Teach

Assuming students lack a skill or strategy because of their age or grade level is a real time stealer. Before you spend days on "commas in a series" because it is in the fourth-grade curriculum, look at your students' writing to see if most are already using that kind of comma with confidence. You can focus on those who aren't in a writing conference, or in a small-group "comma club," and move on to more engaging topics in your minilessons. Also, keep consistent notes as you confer, as you read students' work, and as you listen in on their conversations with each other about what they are writing. Ask yourself often, "What do my students *need* to know for support as writers?" And be ready for surprises. You might just hear a student who concerns you actually *teaching* a partner how to make a better beginning to their story.

Value Writing over Time as Powerful Preparation for Standardized Tests

Children cannot possibly do well on a fourth-grade writing test if they start working on writing in the fourth grade. A joyful practice of writing should begin in pre-K if possible and continue every year throughout a K–12 education. In addition, children will do best in a writing test situation if they have spent years practicing the challenging work of composing in different genres about topics and ideas close to their hearts for appreciative audiences of peers and adults. With lots of experience, students learn how to think about a topic, even a prompted one; to quickly plan how their writing can go; to draft and revise; and to edit for mistakes. Many teachers trust that daily writing workshops offer students the richest foundation for a standardized writing test, setting aside three to four weeks before the test for students to study and practice its particular form and expectations.

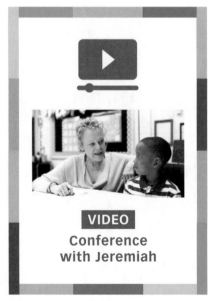

VIDEO
Conference with Jeremiah

take a bow!

Books we love that talk about time in the writing workshop:

Time for Meaning: Crafting Literate Lives in Middle and High School, by Randy Bomer.

The Writing Workshop: Working Through the Hard Parts (And They're All Hard Parts), by Katie Wood Ray.

Benefits of Breaking Out of the "Bubble"

The longer you spend inside the structure and activity of the writing workshop, the more often organic opportunities will arise for your students to write in what Randy Bomer (2011) has called "caught moments—sudden, unplanned opportunistic writing sessions" (59). While we encourage a simple, consistent structure for teaching and learning about writing, we also know that writers appreciate spontaneity. Consider, for example, how a beautiful day, or the approach of a storm, might inspire writers. You might take ten or twenty minutes to walk and look, listen, and feel, or to sit somewhere different (even the sidewalk works!) to write. Or for a new perspective, perhaps your students could write in other spots in the school building—the library, hallway, or another classroom. Here are some other opportunities to catch some writing time outside writing workshop:

- on Friday afternoons

- as soft starts each morning

- as gentle endings to each afternoon

- as a literacy workstation.

Writing Workshop and Multilingual Students

Students who speak and write in languages other than English bring linguistic tools, knowledge, and strengths to their learning of this additional language. Just imagine the boundary crossings our students make between languages—the brain power needed to understand the English in our minilessons; then translate from Spanish, Chinese, Arabic, or Hmong to English; and then form those letters (which for some languages is an entirely different writing system) into words and sentences, and then into genre forms. It is mind-boggling.

Multilingual students need blocks of time, every single day, to practice speaking and writing in English. They need time to write whole and authentic texts: memoirs, picture books, petitions, songs, and more that capture their expertise and build their confidence—what they know a lot about and what they love—not just vocabulary worksheets or grammar exercises that capture neither their love nor their expertise. If we don't force English upon them, and especially if we don't punish or belittle their approximations, eventually we will see more and more English appear. You can also try these ways to support students as they write:

- Invite students to write in the language that is most comfortable

for them, at least at first. And then, as Deborah K. Palmer and Ramón Antonio Martínez (2016) suggest, "allow—even encourage—code switching," because moving between languages is a normal and intelligent practice among multilinguals (382).

- Offer drawing as a way to anchor a story, idea, or memory, and then move from drawing to a letter or word label, and eventually to a sentence or two, and so on.

- Some students *speak* English more comfortably than they write it. Invite students to say their writing into a recording device, replay it, and then write what they can from what they hear.

A multilingual student uses art and words to craft a graphic story.

> **What we do with time is what we do with our lives. When we are 'unable' to spend time on what we most value, it is because we have not found a clarity of purpose.**
>
> **RANDY BOMER**, 1995

take a bow!

Here are some great resources for working with multilingual students in the writing workshop:

The May 2016 issue of the NCTE journal *Language Arts*, "Biliteracy in Schools and Communities," contains a who's who of researchers showcasing their latest thinking on supporting multilingual students.

From Ideas to Words: Writing Strategies for English Language Learners, by Tasha Tropp Laman.

Reading, Writing, and Talk: Inclusive Teaching Strategies for Diverse Learners, K–2, by Marianna Souto-Manning and Jessica Martell.

Choice

part
two

Suppose you simply invited young writers into a room loaded with different kinds and sizes of paper and every type of pencil, marker, paintbrush, and word processing device and you said, "Write whatever you want!" What do you think would happen? What would children write about, and how would they write it? The answer: what and how children will write—when left to their own decision making—is as expansive as their imaginations.

Turn the page to see how a variety of writers responded to the invitation "Write whatever you want" and chose writing projects we would never have even thought to assign them—like lawn mowing, complete with green colored pencil visuals to demonstrate how to cut different patterns in the grass!

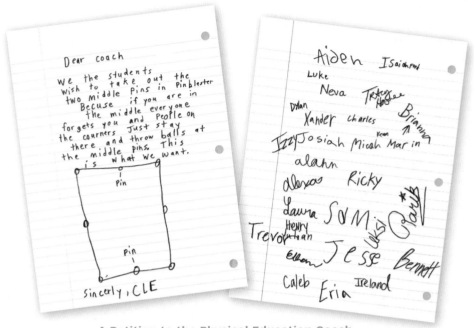

**A Petition to the Physical Education Coach
Advocating for a Change of Rules in a Popular Game**

A Poem on Watercolor Background

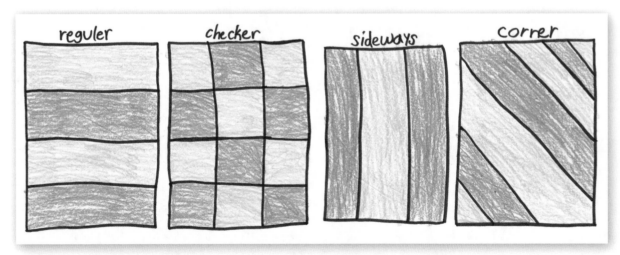

Sketches of Patterns for Mowing Grass (by a Student Who Has His Own Lawn-Mowing Business)

A Picture Book About "Animals Getting Married"

An All-About Book, "Rats That Are Cute"

This kind of choice—of what to write about and how to write it—is the second essential foundation of writing workshop. As teachers, we want our students to "ache with caring," as Mem Fox (1993, 2) perfectly describes the act of writing for authentic purposes. We know that young people write longer and with more joy when they can write about what fills their child-worlds and hearts. They are also open to learning how to write better because they care so much about sharing their writing with others who need to be able to understand their stories, their editorial rants, their instructions for building Lego space stations.

But when we think about choice, it's also important to remember that all writing consists of one decision, or choice, after another. From the initial intention to put marks on the page to the title and dedication, and *everything* in between, a writer is making decisions, making choices. We don't give students choices just so writing will be more enjoyable (though we take delight in our students' joy); students need to learn to "intend their own acts" (Bomer 1995, 41), and learning how to choose is the essence of the *curriculum* of writing. Easily half of our minilessons offer options and strategies for how writers make choices. "Which topic? Which genre or form? How long? How do I start? What tone? Am I finished?"

Understanding Decision Making

To understand the significance of learning to choose in learning how to write well, imagine four very different writers embarking on four pieces of writing:

- a kindergartner writing about werewolves

- a fifth grader writing about summers spent playing in a rec center basketball league

- a twenty-something salesperson who's just attended a trade show and needs to write a report on what they learned for work

- a thirty-something dad with a parenting blog starting a new post on surviving mealtime with toddlers

Now consider just *some* of the decisions each of these very different writers needs to make:

What will I write about?

Having a topic, regardless of whether you chose it or it was assigned, is not the same as knowing what you will write about. Out of everything you *could* write about this topic, what *will* you write about?

What genre or form best serves my topic and purpose?

Sometimes the genre or form is part of the task, but often writers must decide. Poems about werewolves or a book that provides information? A memoir about summer basketball or an op-ed on the need for funding youth sports programs?

Is there anything I need to do before I start writing?

Often, writers need to write to explore an idea and find out what they think and know already. They may need to gather information or read mentor texts in the genre they've chosen.

Who am I writing this for? And why—what's my purpose?

The answer to almost every other question leads back to audience and purpose.

About how long will my writing be? How much space do I have to say what I (or the topic) needs to say?

Sometimes this is totally up to the writer, and sometimes there are length parameters a writer must follow, for example, the trade show report must be five hundred words.

When should I start writing?

In writing workshops students are always writing, but outside school this decision has everything to do with when the writing is due and how much time you think it will take.

Should I think through the parts of this first and make some kind of plan, or start writing and see where it goes?

This decision has to do with length, the nature of the content, and personal writing processes.

How do I start? What's my lead?

So much rides on a good beginning—you want to entrance your reader immediately.

What comes next? And next?

This decision lies between every sentence, every paragraph, every section. What will help the piece make sense and hold the reader's attention?

Should I use this word or that word?

Almost every noun, verb, metaphor, and bit of dialogue represents a deliberate choice that can affect both tone and message.

Have I given my reader enough information, description, and elaboration to understand my meaning?

This question drives the decision to leave something as is or revise it.

Does this *sound* good?

Sound is another consideration, and it also affects the decision to leave something as is or revise it.

Do I need to get someone else to read it and give me feedback on sense and sound?

Writers choose whether to trust their own judgment or seek advice.

Does this follow language and punctuation conventions?

Writers choose to edit carefully for conventions—or not.

Am I finished?

This is not an easy decision for most writers to make. Sometimes a publishing deadline answers it for them.

What can I do to make this look good before I get it to my audience?

Going public with a finished piece of writing involves myriad decisions about presentation.

Now, the five-year-old writing about werewolves may not know he has all these decisions to make, but that's what teaching is for—and to show him he has options for each one. Over time, as he makes choices again and again in writing, and as he talks about those choices with his teacher and his classmates, he'll come to see himself as a particular kind of writer, and he'll learn to say with confidence, "I'm the kind of writer who . . ."

From decades of research and practice by writing teachers around the world, we know that students need (and crave) the opportunity to know themselves in this way and to show us what they are able to do independently. What more could we want than to nourish the writers within each of our students and help them develop awareness and responsibility for who they are as writers, what they need, and when they need it?

Cruz decides to insert a speech bubble in his werewolves book called "Legendary."

> 66
>
> **The writing workshop is an impressive machine with all sort of conveyors, pulleys, bells and whistles. What fuel makes it work so well? Student choice. Remove that and the big apparatus quickly grinds to a halt.**
>
> **RALPH FLETCHER,** 2018

Truthfully, letting go of control and allowing students to make so many decisions about what and how to write can make us feel uncomfortable. We wonder: "If my students choose their own topics and forms of writing, how can I be sure each child is mastering the grade-level standards? How will I ever manage to help with their research if they each have their own topic? How will I know what to teach if everyone is writing something different?" But we're not surrendering our control when we offer students choice; instead, we're creating conditions for them to show us what they *need* us to teach them as we tap into their knowledge, their intense obsessions, and their deep cares and concerns.

VIDEO
Conference with Jalen

But What About ...?

I worry that my students will stare at blank pages if I don't directly instruct and manage their writing.

Too often, this worry causes teachers to determine what and how children will write by using prompts, activities, formulas, and look-alike products. But if you micromanage the whole process, kids can become overwhelmed by the numerous and sometimes-confusing language and formatting rules. Many children will be so busy trying to "do it right" that they will fear making mistakes (never a good context for learning anything). They may also become bored writing about topics they don't care about. So, in addition to the fact that students aren't learning anything about the decision-making process when you micromanage, writing can also become a burden of rule following instead of a process of discovery.

A student plans in her notebook . . .

. . . before drafting an adventure chapter book.

Choice Matters

When students have lots of choices about what they will write about and how they will write it, there are many benefits.

Instructional Benefits

- Choice taps into what kids know and care about in the world, which gives their writing voice and makes them excited to produce more and to make their writing the best it can be.

- Centering students' language and experience through topic choice provides an environment for culturally relevant teaching (Ladson-Billings 1995).

- Choice offers comfortable entry points into the world of writing for all different ages and kinds of writers.

- Students no longer need to contort their thinking to figure out something to write in response to someone else's external prompt.

- Teachers no longer need to search for "fun" topics and clever formulas that will excite students to write.

- When students write about topics they know and care about, it provides a more authentic assessment of their strengths.

Social-emotional Benefits

- Children and teachers learn about the people they share space with each day, creating an intimate and compassionate community. What are their stories? What makes them who they are?

- Kids learn their voices matter, and that what they think and write is safe in this community.

- Writers feel a strong sense of power, energy, and investment in work that comes from their own minds and hearts.

- Students become independent writers and problem solvers as they practice processes that work for them.

- Young writers enjoy the same privilege enjoyed by published authors—the ability to write exactly what they want to write, the way they want to write it.

Possibilities for Maximizing Student Choice

Let's think now about all the ways you might give your students more choice in the writing workshop. As we consider these possibilities, remember that we believe that if time, choice, and response were *all* you gave students, they would become enthusiastic, fluent, skillful writers after a year of writing every single day in school. However, we'll assume that you are also teaching them minilessons every day about topics like why people write, how to find mentor authors to imitate, how to build tension in a narrative scene, and how to make a text ready to publish. Choice sets the tone for joy and purpose in this teaching. It's the mother of all anticipatory sets for lesson planning: "Kids, take this teaching I'm about to deliver back to all your wonderful writing projects and decide how to use it!" With that appetizing offer, you hook them, and then you deliver the main dish—explicit instruction in how to write well. Elaboration techniques, revision strategies, and especially editing are much easier for students to try out if they care about the topic they have chosen or the story they're trying to tell.

Some of the possibilities for choice we offer here might feel more radical than you are ready to try. Not a problem! As long as you allow

Writing About Healthy Food, a Student-Generated Topic

students the most important choices of all—what to write about and how to write it—you'll be giving love to one of the three "bigs" of the writing workshop.

Topics

One problem with writing prompts is that young writers may not have a single thing to say about them, so they write empty, meaningless responses. Or they may have plenty to say, but they struggle to fit their ideas or language into standardized formulas that live inside schools, but not the world (Bomer 2015). Students may become frustrated, bored, or even resentful when they are required to invent clever things to write in response to prompts like "Imagine you are a turkey. Persuade the family that is about to cook you for Thanksgiving dinner to let you live."

When they only respond to prompts, students do not listen enough to their own thinking, feeling, remembering, and wondering about the world. In high school, and especially when they begin college coursework, students will be asked repeatedly to write their opinions, to argue for or against, to elaborate and provide evidence, to *think* in writing.

There is hope, however! When children write about topics they've chosen, they are in comfortable, engaging territory. Ideas, memories, and descriptions flow more easily. They are better able to focus on logical organization, style moves, sentence structures, prediction of a reader's questions, and elaboration to create richly textured writing that is full of voice, because it is, in fact, their actual voice.

Even if you are studying how to write in a particular genre—such as all-about books in first grade or feature articles in fourth grade—students can still choose their own topics. The success of the writing does not hinge on the topic, which could be anything from climate change to a certain puffy, spicy, fried cheese snack. In fact, almost any topic in the world can be framed to fit almost any genre, so once you know how much choice matters, it makes sense that students should *always* choose their own topics.

VIDEO
The Importance of Topic Choice

But What About ...?

What if I have students who write about the same topic (video games, sports, animals) every day?

There are several ways to think about this question:

- Celebrate that these students are like many professional writers who have passions and interests and write about them again and again in different ways.

- Invite these students to write about their obsession in a variety of genres (poem, essay, story, information) and for diverse audiences: younger children; friends who "get it"; the president of the United States; readers who did not even know or care about this topic until they read this student's writing.

- Remember that having a topic is not the same thing as "what I will write about this topic." A writer who knows things about a topic has content knowledge that could go in many different directions and lead to lots of different writing—all about the same general subject.

- Trust that these students will find other things to write about across the school year. They might be inspired by peers to try other topics, or they might get ideas from reading. And you can gently invite them to try other subjects after you have spent time together and listened to them talk about their interests both in and out of school.

Students who are new to writing workshop, especially if they come from other schools where writing instruction did not happen or was always prompted, might resist your joyous invitation to "write about whatever you want!" They might be afraid to take a risk, or they might simply have no idea how to begin writing "whatever they want" as no one has taught them strategies for doing that. Either way, moving these students forward will take time, trust, and demonstration from you and from more comfortable writers in the class. Here are some ideas to get you started with that teaching:

- Talk often about why and how students are choosing their topics. All you need is for one student to have an idea for writing in mind, and then you can ask questions like these:

  Where did you get this idea?

  Have you ever written about this before? If you have, how did you decide you had more to say about it?

  Have you read about this topic? Experienced it?

  How did you know this was the topic you most wanted to write about?

- Develop a chart documenting the ideas and topics students are exploring.

- Support topic choice by wondering where writers might have gotten ideas for the texts you are reading. You may not know for sure, but teach students to think about where writers' ideas and motivations might have come from when they read.

- If you are starting a whole-class genre study, spend some time first just looking at lots of examples and talking about the topics you see writers have chosen.

- Read authors' notes and book jackets to see if they explain how an idea came to be. Search for authors' webpages, where many authors write or explain in videos where they get their ideas and offer advice for young writers.

- If you've been teaching writing workshop for several years, you might invite students from previous classes to talk to your current students about how they got ideas for writing.

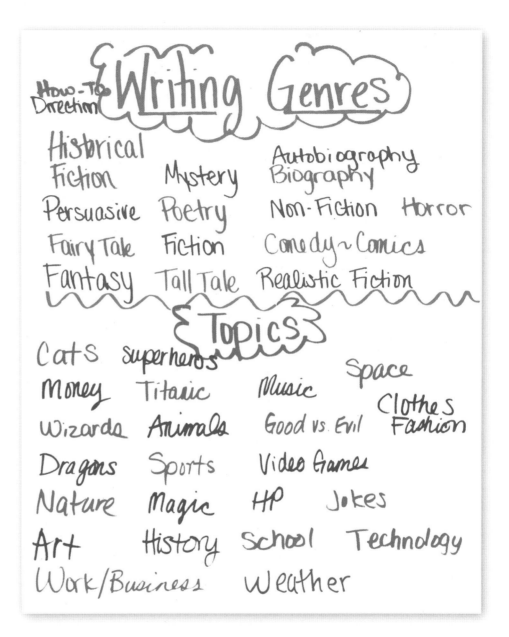

Writing Notebooks:
A Tool for Finding Topics

For writers, the world is a daily feast of possibilities for poems, articles, stories, and plays. Writers listen and observe, and they document things that interest them in notebooks they carry everywhere. They record wonderings and descriptions of the world that either feed their current projects or could become the inspiration for a new project. They also play with ideas, try out different word choices, practice dialogue, plan, and think about their ongoing projects.

The best container we know for helping students in third grade and up capture all this thinking is a writing notebook. We invite students to keep a notebook and to "live like writers," listening, observing, and jotting down the things that draw their attention. We ask them to write and sketch about their memories and passions. Then we ask them to choose what they want to turn into a writing project from the material they gathered. The gathering is crucial because it shows kids that if they are alive, they are wealthy with material—they simply need to record that richness so they will always have plenty to choose from.

If your students keep writing notebooks, talk often about what they are recording inside them because this talk is so generative. Students get ideas when they see and hear what others are doing, so let them share entries with each other in partnerships and small groups. When you share as a whole class, make charts of the kinds of entries and ideas students are finding. If you embark on a genre study, talk about the kinds of things students will need to gather in their notebooks to feed this new genre.

Writing in Notebooks ⬇

VIDEO
Writing in Notebooks

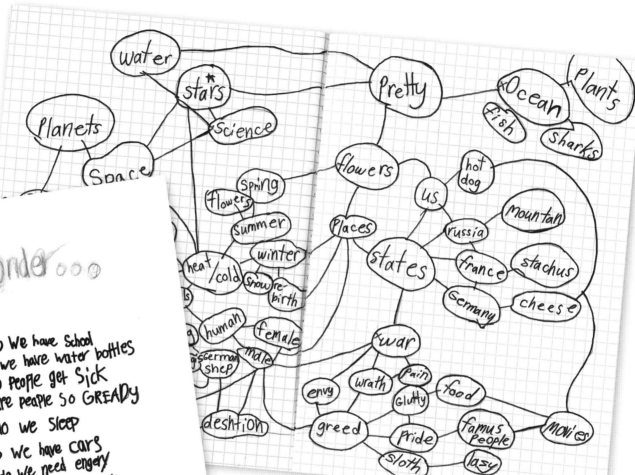

Students' Writing in Notebooks

Sometimes students can be so overwhelmed with topic choices that they are paralyzed, but responding to that problem with a writing prompt doesn't help children problem solve and grow into independence. Instead, demonstrate strategies like these for making choices—ways to filter through possibilities and narrow down to topics kids really want or need to write about.

• Create and maintain a web or a heart map (Heard 2016), or a list of open-ended invitations to respond to (see Online Resources, Bomer 2015), or some other list of favorite topics you can revisit whenever you feel stuck.

• Choose three favorites from any of the lists and write for five minutes about each of those things.

• Reread your notebook and look for something you could write about again (perhaps your go-to topic).

• Find something you jotted down quickly in your notebook and write more about it.

• Write to explore what is nagging at you.

• Ask a trusted partner what they think you could write.

• Look out the window and write about whatever catches your eye: a bus, a boarded-up apartment building, a woman walking a dog, a meadow.

Thinking About Beginning Writers

Young children are the keenest observers of the world around them, so you may wonder why we recommend writing notebooks only for grades three and up. First, we feel strongly that beginning writers need to make their marks on all kinds of surfaces—recycled greeting cards, graph paper, notepads, scrapbooking paper—and invent exciting ways to create and use writing. Second, to use a notebook efficiently, you have to write fast enough to "capture" your thinking. Most beginning writers aren't yet able to do that, and even if they can do it, they won't be able to reread much of what they've written, so it's not that useful. Until they have developed fluency, consider helping beginning writers capture ideas they find in the world with talk. Ask them about interesting things they have seen or thought about away from school. Encourage them to bring in objects that hold meaning that they can talk and write about. Go for walks outside together and practice observing and noticing.

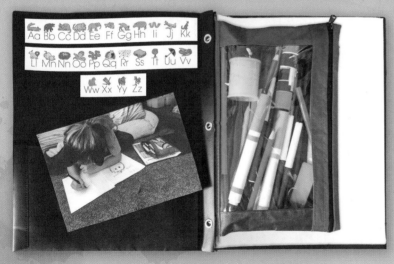

A Folder with Materials to Support Independence in the Primary Grades

Evaluating Topics

In their notebooks, students don't need to think a lot about whether a topic is "good enough" to write about—they can always move on to something else. But when it's time to choose a topic for a project that will go through the entire writing process, that's a bigger decision. Students who are not used to generating their own ideas sometimes choose topics that aren't particularly meaningful for them and their energy for writing quickly dissolves. Also, choosing a topic, even if it's a good one, doesn't always mean it will be the best fit for a certain genre or appropriate for a targeted audience.

Choosing topics *well* is critical to students' success as writers, so with questions like these we show students how to consider topics before they make a final decision.

Is my topic too broad?

A topic like "how to play flag football," for many writers, is too broad to manage. Instead, the writer could zoom in on one aspect of playing the game, such as how to pass the ball effectively. Or a student might be writing one of those infamous narratives that go on for ages, has too many characters, and loses its focus. This writer may need to make a storyboard, cut whole characters, or trim pages of text.

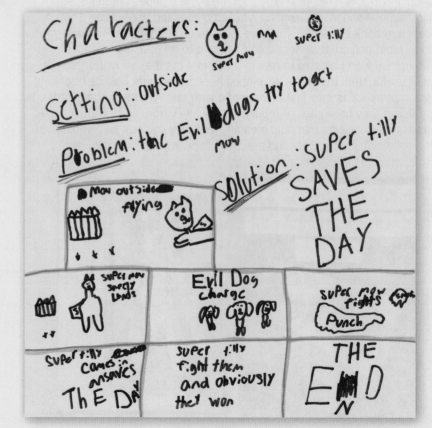

A student uses a storyboard as a prewriting strategy.

Would this topic require me to do extensive research? If so, am I up for that research?

Realistically, a student may be very interested in a topic—the history of the microchip, for instance—but not have the time, energy, or available resources to write a feature article about it. Considering this question *before* they settle on a topic can help students avoid frustration.

Does this topic lend itself well to the audience I have in mind?

Inviting students to imagine their readers and what they might need is powerful writing instruction. Sometimes, an early topic choice does not match the intended audience. For example, a fifth grader writing a picture book for her first-grade brother drafts a story about a character falling in love and being rejected by a cute science lab partner and then realizes the book is more appropriate for a middle school reader. Again, considering the question of audience *before* you settle on a topic is helpful.

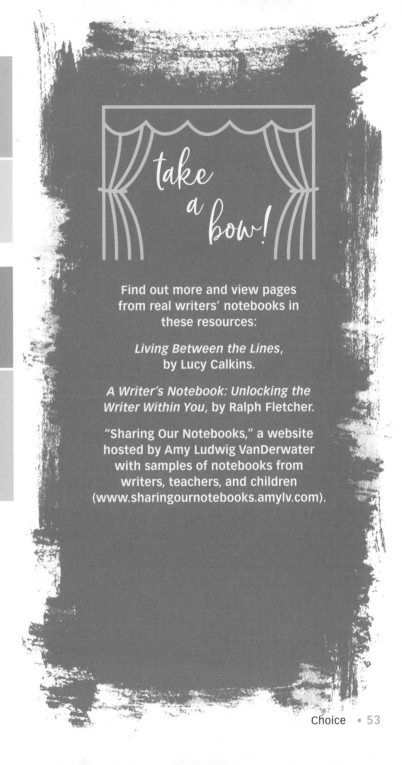

take a bow!

Find out more and view pages from real writers' notebooks in these resources:

Living Between the Lines, by Lucy Calkins.

A Writer's Notebook: Unlocking the Writer Within You, by Ralph Fletcher.

"Sharing Our Notebooks," a website hosted by Amy Ludwig VanDerwater with samples of notebooks from writers, teachers, and children (www.sharingournotebooks.amylv.com).

TIME, CHOICE, **AND** RESPONSE **IN ACTION**

Response

Jennie's writing partners and classmates often choose to read graphic texts, and Jennie is "famous" for fabulous, detailed, and colorful illustrations.

Choice

It's clear from Jennie's topics list that she loves fantasy and art. Writing workshop gave her the time and support to develop her writing and illustrating with a topic she has so much to imagine about and elaborate.

Time

From listing possible topics, to thinking about how the story could go, to sketches in the margins, to drafting, revising, and illustrating the final, full-color text, the process Jennie used to write her graphic fantasy book unfolded over multiple days.

fantasy
topics
- Wich
- mermaids
- magic croyn
- Princess
- Dragons
- the magic flower
- the talking Light
- fairys
- girl With Wings
- Uincorn

dragons course
The girl Wakes up in the morning and sees a dragon in her bedroom and the Dragon disapeer and Left a chest and girl Whent to see the chest and girl Fell in the chest and saw a village full of dragons and the girl thoght the snow was Fire but it Was not it Was Just narmall and all the dragons stopd What they Where doing and SCEAMD out Fire and Lucy said dragons are not real right" I'm I dreaming snap out of it Lucy.
to find 10 gems. With a
magic

dragons course
Last night, my parunts tuck me in for bed. I said "good night". When I fell aSleep my dog came in and culed With me. I Woke up at the middle of the night a baby dragon Was in my room and I got scard. then the baby dragon disapear. A chest fell on the floor. Lucy Whent to go see the chest....SHE FELL IN THE CHEST! Lucy Scereamed so loud the dragons can hear her from the Village. Lucy fell on the ground. the dragons stop What they Where doing and Scereamd out fire! in the air Like ribbins. Lucy Said "Are dragons real or What. the King dragon Said "Who dares gose in my Kingdom" everybody Whent to hide but except "a human" said a dragon "Shhh" said a dr "if you Want to escape you hav to find gems for me" said the King dragon. Lucy. the King dragon send 2 big With Lucy. Lucy Went in the anchan forist With the big dragon. So Walked and Walked for miels but found this werid animal that Was rainbow and it had Wings and a horn What can that be a..."UINCORN" Said Lucy. "Yeah of cores that is a uincorn" Said the big dragon.

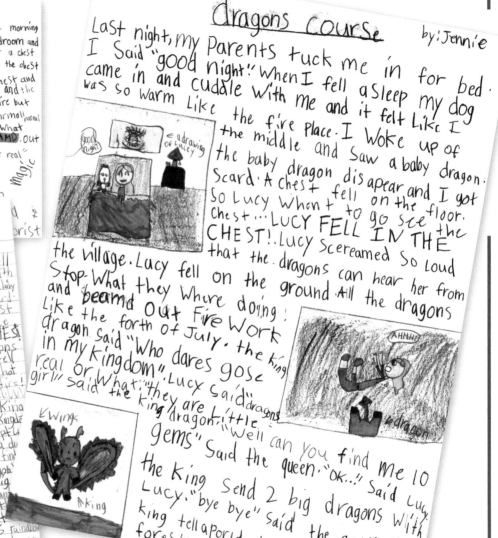
dragons course   by: Jennie
Last night, my Parents tuck me in for bed. I said "good night". When I fell asleep my dog came in and cuddle with me and it felt Like I was so warm Like the fire Place. I Woke up of the middle and Saw a baby dragon. the baby dragon disapear and I got scard. A chest fell on the floor. so Lucy Whent to go see the chest....LUCY FELL IN THE CHEST! Lucy scereamed so loud that the dragons can hear her from the village. Lucy fell on the ground. All the dragons stop What they Where doing and beamd out Fire Work Like the forth of July. the king dragon said "Who dares gose in my Kingdom" Lucy said "dragons real or What" "they are Little" said the king dragon. "Well can you find me 10 gems" said the queen. "OK.." Said Lucy. the King send 2 big dragons With Lucy. "bye bye" said the queen. the king tellaPorted Lucy to the enchanted forest. and the big dragons. they saw this

Materials

Most practiced writers have serious preferences for writing materials. For instance, one writer may get a queasy stomach writing with a dull pencil, while another writer insists on writing longhand on yellow legal pads with an extra-fine Pilot Precise V5 rolling-ball black-ink pen. When it comes to materials, writers know what they like—and what they don't.

Materials often make a big difference in student writing as well. Forcing a child to write on college-ruled notebook paper simply because they're in third grade, for instance, may turn them into a reluctant writer. This reluctance may have nothing to do with their knowledge, talent, or willingness to engage, but instead may involve a fear and dislike of so many thin blue lines. A super-bright fifth grader who cannot read their own handwriting and so refuses to write more than two sentences may become the next Neil Gaiman when you introduce them to a computer keyboard. A basket filled with blank, unused greeting cards or a giant piece of chart paper could be just the invitation for a kindergartner to joyously write.

The thing is, materials *matter* to writers, and if you fill your workshop with a variety of paper, writing utensils, and electronic devices, you'll almost certainly watch your students' energy and joy for writing bubble over. The more material choices you give students, the more opportunities they have to explore and discover what works best for them. Here are some possibilities to explore on the right:

- different types of paper (blank, several lines under a large picture box, lined, colored, different shapes, card stock, poster-sized, blank books)
- writing notebooks
- clipboards
- writing utensil(s)
  - → markers (thin, thick, permanent, washable)
  - → pencils
  - → pens
  - → crayons
  - → watercolor, tempera paints
  - → keyboard and word processor, tablet, typewriter, whiteboard
  - → computer with internet access
- writing tools
  - → tape
  - → glue
  - → staplers
  - → sticky notes
  - → highlighters
  - → art paper to make book covers
  - → dictionaries
  - → thesaurus

GRAPH PAPER   NOTEBOOK PAPER   BLANK PAPER

PENCILS   EXPOS   WHITEBOARD ERASERS

PENS   SCISSORS

HIGHLIGHTERS   GLUE   MEASURING TAPES

create

Watch out for erasing! Many kids erase constantly, using it as a stalling tactic or because they fear making mistakes. Teach children that mistakes are part of the process, so erasing, at least in the writing notebook or in drafts, is unnecessary. They can just draw a single line through a word or letter if they want to change it.

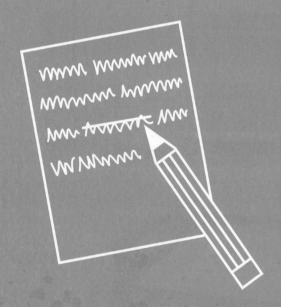

As you observe students at work and confer with them, pay attention to the material choices they are making. You may see opportunities to "teach into" what you see and help them make different or even better choices. From time to time, talk together as a whole class about how students are using materials so students might be inspired to try out what their peers use.

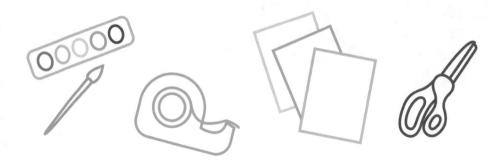

But What About...?

With all these materials available, what if I have students who spend all their time sketching or drawing?

Art, like writing, is an act of composing and a process of making decisions about (among other things) topic, shapes, color, texture, size, technique, materials, what to elaborate, and what to leave out. We can celebrate that these students are like Yuyi Morales, Mo Willems, Raina Telgemeier, and other famous writers who make graphic texts and get their ideas from drawing. We can encourage them to use drawing as a rehearsal for writing and show them how to move from one to the other. We can also direct them to mentor texts that include art and words—for example, picture books and graphic novels—and be open to students creating graphic texts during writing workshop.

An Excerpt from a Student's Graphic Novel "Captain Obvious and the Wipeout of the Wretched Worm"

Thinking About Beginning Writers

Our youngest writers will convey lots of their meaning through their art, so it's important that they have materials to support this meaning making. Encourage them to be intentional and actually compose with their illustrations, and then show them how to add writing to their art. Ask, "Can you find one thing in your drawing that you could label (with a letter, word, phrase)?" Move from label to sentence, to chunk of text, to a three- or five-page stapled book or to any other type of paper kids feel confident writing on. And be sure to save young children's writing over time (hanging file folders work great for this) so you can see their tremendous growth unfold.

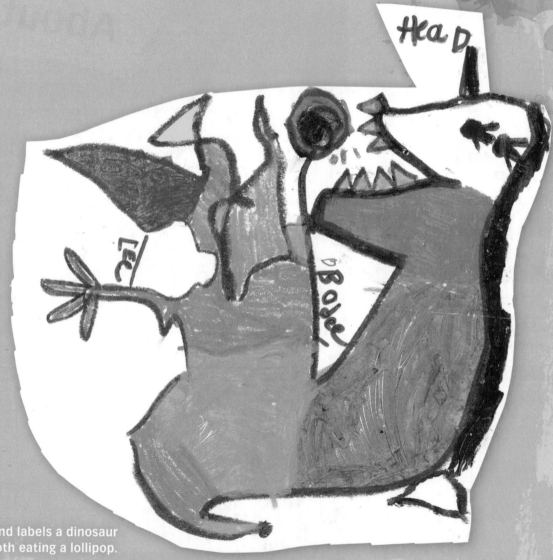

A pre-K child draws and labels a dinosaur with a wiggly tooth eating a lollipop.

Work Spaces

Writers work in all kinds of spaces: on a couch, in a bed, at a coffee shop, in a cabin in the woods, at a library, in an airplane seat, under a tree, and sometimes even at a desk. Some need a quiet, uncluttered space; others like to be surrounded by noise and activity. Some look for a place that inspires them; others just write to get it done and can do it almost anywhere. Writers write where they are comfortable and know they can get a lot of work done, and inside our classrooms our students should be able to do that too.

If you teach students to ask, "What kind of space do I *need* as a writer?" and "Where can I get my best writing done?" you can then consider how to use the space in your classroom to best support them. Students might want to write

- in a special chair or on a couch
- on the floor (on a rug, on giant pillows, with clipboards)
- at a table or desk
- in the hallway
- in close proximity to other writers or in a space all their own

A Classroom with Open Spaces Where Students Can Choose to Write

In addition to space, you might also talk with students about the writing environment and whether there are things you could do to make it more conducive to their writing work. For example:

- Lighting. Would it help to turn off the fluorescents overhead in favor of softer table and floor lamps?

- Music. Would calming, beautiful sounds in the background help you focus?

- Sustenance. Would it help you to have snacks and water while you're writing?

- Talking. Do you get distracted when you hear other people talking? If so, can we create quiet spaces and talking spaces?

Students Choosing Different Places to Write

> Children learn through making choices. They search their lives and interests, make a choice, and write. Some of the decisions are poor ones. But with help, they regain control, make better choices. Above all, they learn to control a subject, limit it, persuade, sequence information, change their language . . . all to satisfy their own voices, not the voices of others.

DONALD GRAVES, 1983B, 31

Genres or Kinds of Writing

While you will often study and write in certain genres together as a class, there should also be innumerable opportunities for students to choose the kind or form of writing they wish to try. In conferences, if you ask kids what genre their writing seems to be leaning toward, you can help steer them toward genres that suit their topics. For example, a student might be writing a list of facts about the tons of plastic that clog our oceans as a poem, when the tone might be better served by an editorial or TED Talk. Or imagine a student who wants to

- describe a memory or feeling using lean, essential words or a surprising metaphor in a poem

- teach other kids facts about the necessity of snakes in our ecosystem (so they will not fear them) in a feature article or all-about book

- share the untold stories of immigrants' contributions to the United States in a keynote speech, or a mini-documentary with photos, music, and narration

The possibilities are endless. Students can choose from any genre they know that will best serve their intentions. If they know it as readers, they can try it as writers! And if there's a genre

Student Begins Drafting a Movie Script

that students don't know, but you think would serve them well, you can get some examples—what we often call "mentor texts"—and show them. Here are some common forms and genres in the world of writing that young people can write gorgeously:

- picture books (a container for any genre)
- short stories
- essays
- poems
- informational (teaching) texts
- feature articles
- editorials
- reviews
- speeches
- instructional and procedural (how-to) texts
- graphic texts (comics, short stories)
- websites
- photo essays
- ad copy
- TED Talks
- YouTube videos, podcasts
- TV and film scripts
- song lyrics

When they have the freedom to do so, some teachers plan a whole year of teaching that is not genre specific, though they may encourage students to try out different forms in order to stretch and grow their writing prowess.

What Is a Mentor Text?

A mentor text is a good example of a kind of writing students are learning how to make. Mentor texts often come from the published world of writing, but they may also be texts written by other students or the teacher. It's usually best if students see multiple examples of mentor texts so they have multiple possibilities in mind when they begin writing their own.

VIDEO

Teaching a Minilesson with Mentor Texts

Other teachers, who structure most of the year around whole-class studies of genres, set aside routine time—every Friday, for instance—for students to work on writing projects in genres they've chosen. Often, kids work on these projects over a long period of time, and they're excited to return to them each week. Other teachers plan for shorter units of study (in between longer genre studies) where kids can explore any kind of writing they want to make and the teaching is not tied to genre—for example, a two-week focus on revision strategies or a one-week study of the sentence and its varieties.

Preserving Choice in a Genre Study

There is real value in studying a genre together as a class, though this means students have to write in that genre, so they lose that critical choice that can be so motivating and engaging for them as writers (Glover 2020, 3). However, we can be intentional in our planning to ensure students have a wealth of choices *inside* a genre study. Here are some ideas:

- Give students plenty of time and support to find personally meaningful topics that make sense for the genre you are studying. Don't rush this stage. Look at examples in mentor texts, talk about a variety of topic ideas, and

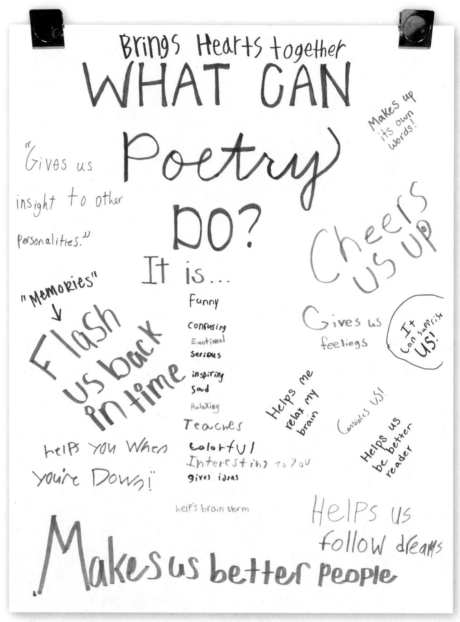

Recording the *Qualities* of the Genre During a Study

generate lists of possibilities in notebooks.

- Be sure the mentor texts you choose represent a range of styles and ways to approach writing in the genre, so students have many options for *how* they will write.

- Offer a range of strategies for planning, drafting, and revising so students can choose the ones they think best fit their intentions.

- Offer a range of options for how students can publish their finished work: allow them to use different layouts and visual features; give them the opportunity to record their work as a podcast or publish it digitally online.

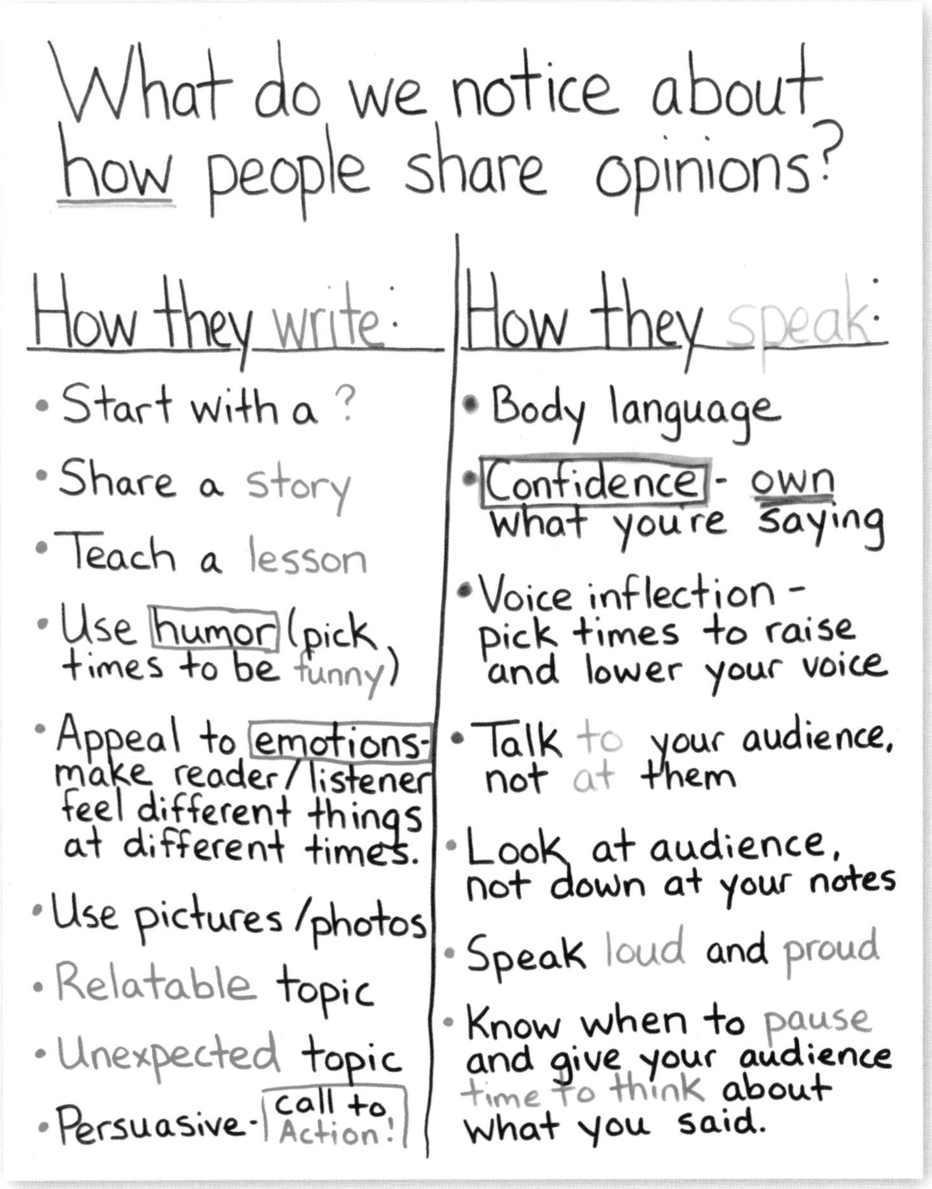

What do we notice about how people share opinions?

How they write:

- Start with a ?
- Share a story
- Teach a lesson
- Use humor (pick times to be funny)
- Appeal to emotions- make reader/listener feel different things at different times.
- Use pictures/photos
- Relatable topic
- Unexpected topic
- Persuasive- call to Action!

How they speak:

- Body language
- Confidence - own what you're saying
- Voice inflection - pick times to raise and lower your voice
- Talk to your audience, not at them
- Look at audience, not down at your notes
- Speak loud and proud
- Know when to pause and give your audience time to think about what you said.

Another Example of Recording the *Qualities* of the Genre During a Study

The Writing Process

Writing is a recursive activity, with stops and starts, revisions, and edits. For seasoned writers in the midst of drafting, this all happens almost simultaneously—it's not a linear, step-by-step process. As teachers, we need to demonstrate the distinct aspects of the writing process and then give our students time to practice the strategies we show them. Ultimately, though, developing writers have to find their own way, so we give them as much control of the process as possible. We try not to hinder or hurry, hoping each child discovers a process for writing that works for them.

Here are some process choices writers make that we can, as often as possible, invite our students to make for themselves:

- how to use the writing notebook for what each writer needs rather than as a prescribed (or corrected or graded) task

- whether to draft on paper or the computer

- how many drafts to produce

- when to meet with a partner or small group for feedback

- what type of feedback the writer needs and when they need it

- what revision strategies to use

- what editing strategies to use.

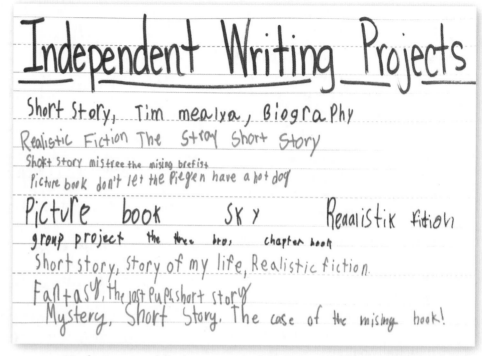

Students record their current independent writing projects.

You can also let your students decide how to pace themselves through all this different process work. You might give them time parameters and then let them manage and navigate the process on their own. A strictly prescribed system tends to produce passive writing machines, who wait for instructions: when to begin, when to revise, when to edit, and when to finish. Instead, the goal is to teach students to work according to a reflective, self-directed sense of when and how to move through the writing process. If your students have never worked like this as writers before, they probably won't do any of this very well *at first*. And that's okay. If you let them go ahead and get started, you will see how to begin teaching them to do it all better.

Social Arrangements

All writers need company—they need to talk through their ideas, and they need other eyes and ears to reflect back what their writing is making readers think and question. We dedicate a whole section of this book to response in the writing workshop, but here we just want to suggest that you can also offer students choices about the social arrangements that support them as writers. See the next page for a few options to consider.

Students might also decide how often they need to talk to others about their writing—requirements will be different for different students. Ask them: "Do you need time every day? A few times a week? Do you want a set time when everyone is sharing, or would it be better if you could meet with a partner any time you *need* to meet? If so, where could we create a space for partners or groups to meet while others are writing?" If you can negotiate a schedule for social work on writing, students will feel like they have more control over the process, though you'll probably need to revisit the schedule periodically to talk about how it's working.

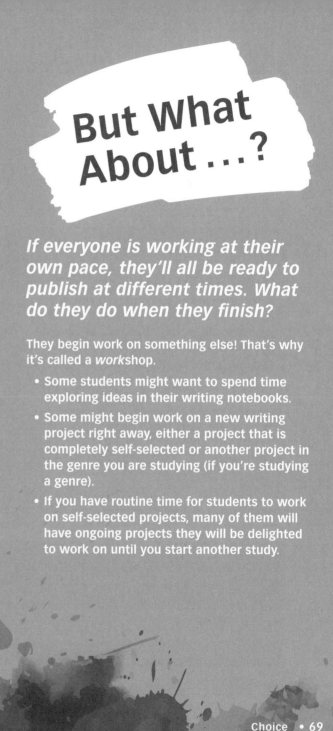

But What About ...?

If everyone is working at their own pace, they'll all be ready to publish at different times. What do they do when they finish?

They begin work on something else! That's why it's called a *work*shop.

- Some students might want to spend time exploring ideas in their writing notebooks.
- Some might begin work on a new writing project right away, either a project that is completely self-selected or another project in the genre you are studying (if you're studying a genre).
- If you have routine time for students to work on self-selected projects, many of them will have ongoing projects they will be delighted to work on until you start another study.

Partnerships

Two writers give each other feedback over time. They may change during the year, but they should stay together long enough to get to know each other's writing preferences and processes.

Small Writing Groups

Four or five students meet regularly to offer feedback and support from multiple perspectives. As in partnerships, it helps for them to stay together long enough to get to know each other as writers.

Collaborative Writing Projects

Students decide to work together on a project and make decisions about *how* they will collaborate.

Conference Requests

In some classrooms, students can sign up when they know they need a conference with the teacher (in addition to the teacher's *planned* conference schedule).

Audiences for Celebrations

Students might decide whom to invite—and why.

Publications

If you show students numerous possibilities to get their writing into the world, they can choose how and where they want to try and publish their work.

Starting with Choice Right from the Start

If you're convinced that it's important for students to have many choices in writing workshop, you may be wondering about the best way to set this up at the beginning of the year. There's not really one answer to this question. Some teachers begin the year with a short study of poetry to set a tone of beautiful writing and to easily teach many features of writing through short texts. Others begin with a genre study of memoir or personal narrative so teachers and students can get to know each other through their writing. Some teachers begin by exploring with students how to live like writers, use a writing notebook, and fill page after page with ideas that can be raw material for any genre study. Still others start the year with self-selected writing projects, inviting students to make any kind of writing they want—another great way to get to know each other's passions and delights. However you start, remember to write alongside your students (perhaps for the first five minutes, before you confer), share your own process with them, and give them choices wherever you can.

Finally, you may be wondering, "Is there anything students *don't* have a choice about in writing workshop?" The answer is yes, and every teacher has to decide what is nonnegotiable. For us, we've decided that students cannot choose

- Whether or not to write (barring illness or an especially fraught day). Everyone writes in this community. That's what we *do* here!

- The beginning and ending of writing workshop time. This is a decision we have to make with consideration for the whole schedule of the school day.

- Whether or not to be kind and constructive in their comments about each other's writing. Kindness makes it possible for humans to live, work, and write together.

Writing Workshop and Multilingual Students

Choice of topic, materials, and form gives language learners the freedom to express what they are able (and willing) to create for now. They should not have to struggle with the additional rules of certain forms on *top* of trying to write in English. They should not feel additional frustration about a prompt they may not understand or have experienced.

Some teachers might worry that choice is not appropriate for children learning English as an additional language because of all the extra instruction that might need to accompany so much decision making. They might offer scaffolds for writing that eliminate writers' choices, such as sentence starters, graphic organizers, or vocabulary lists. However, scaffolds like these isolate language into partial bits and do not reflect language *in use*. Writing whole texts helps multilingual students see the whole of language—how sentences flow into each other to make sense, how a story moves through time, and how paragraphs build upon each other to make meaning.

We believe the best approach for learning how to compose texts in English is for multilingual students to work alongside their peers and to discover, with your help, what makes sense and works best. Here are a few supports you can offer students as they make choices and decisions:

- Provide mentor texts in both a student's first language and English, as often as possible, and allow students to choose which mentor text they would like to try to imitate.

- Allow students to choose when to compose in their first language, when to begin to sprinkle in English words they feel comfortable using, when to begin to use English more liberally, and when to write mostly in English.

- If students need more support to understand the many choices they have, you might simplify their options just a little: this place or that place to sit; pen or pencil; blank or lined paper; one of three possible topics from their "heart map" or list of topics. With each day's experience, they will grow to understand more and more options.

Response

part
three

From the moment of birth, nearly every living thing requires nurturing response from others. See me. Feed me. Comfort me. Love me. Responding to those needs helps living things survive and thrive. Children actively demand attention and appreciation from family members, teachers, and friends. This is how they learn how to be (and not be) in the world. If you have spent any time poolside with a child, you have heard the echoes of "Watch this! Look at me! Did you see that?" bellowing from the water. A simple "Wow!" or "I sure did!" can beam our pride and encouragement. These little voices want to be heard, and they want to know that someone notices their attempts to dive or do a shaky underwater handstand. In these moments, children are looking not for critical commentary but rather a cheer of hope and support. We would be lying if we said we have not felt the same way.

Writers also crave response to their work. They want readers who understand and—hopefully—admire the ideas, emotions, and style moves they have worked hard to turn into a novel, poem, biography, or blog post. As they compose, most writers ask trusted friends and editors for feedback, knowing those responses will directly improve their work. They need another pair or five of eyes to help them find more efficient ways to organize the material, extra ears to hear awkward phrasing, and supportive voices to offer appreciation and constructive criticism of the unfolding material.

For our young writers, having someone responding at the other end of their work gives them a reason to write. The same in-process response that professional writers receive is even more crucial for children, so they may begin to anticipate how readers will react and internalize a sense of audience. If their writing partners are confused, for example, they can revise to help future readers better understand their meaning.

Finally, when students receive response throughout the process of writing, they learn that revision is just a natural part of writing and they need not fear it or try to avoid it. In fact, revision is part of life, isn't it? Imagine if we couldn't tweak our appearance, change our minds, or improve our behaviors. Learning how to give compassionate response and process helpful critique also teaches us how to be in a relationship with others. It teaches us how to speak with kindness and without judgment.

TIME, CHOICE, **AND RESPONSE** IN ACTION

Response

As you might imagine, this essay found an audience beyond the classroom and was shared with older kids and adults who admired David's courage and sensitivity. The feedback made him want to write more.

Choice

Most students would avoid the topic of depression (we hope they know nothing about it). But David said, "I can't breathe while I write if I don't have a choice." He chose to write about this topic and to share with the world a powerful, selfless path to find the light again.

Time

David composed this piece in the last days of his final year in elementary school. We believe that the trust and safety of a whole year in a writing workshop community, led by an appreciative, loving teacher, enabled him to write his truth in this essay.

Help Yourself

In my experience with sadness and depression, I'd say not to live for yourself but for someone else. Help people to make *yourself* feel better. Honestly, life is rough. It doesn't care about you so strive for more. Even if someone close to you died. Even if you were bullied. Be better for *them*. Even when you feel so sad, you'd rather die, keep fighting. I know it's hard to believe, but there is light at the end of this tunnel. And that light can dim, but once you get there, it will take a lot for that light to go out.

Remember how I said in my experience? That's because I do have experience with this kind of sadness. I've been sad for a long time so just trust me, ok?

Even if you really want to give up, just keep pushing. Here's a good way to do it: if not for yourself, think of everyone else! And, if you don't have anyone else, tie yourself to someone...<u>anyone</u>. Help them as much as you can. Help them so you can help yourself not feel worthless. No matter who you are, nobody's worthless.

Now, I'm not you'll be completely better, I'm just saying it will help a little. That's what it did for me, and I hope it will do the same for you. Even if the favors you do aren't for you, they'll make you feel better and BE better! Those favors will help you not feel worthless. Even if it's not for your own gain, you'll still <u>have</u> a gain. Even though those favors aren't for you, they are for you. You just don't know it yet.

Make the world a better place because you're not worthless, so don't think you are. Just keep going because you're worth **something**. You can do **something**! Just keep pushing! For yourself! For them! For the world!

You will always mean something to someone.

Response Matters

In our classrooms, we can create routines and rituals that give our students feedback throughout the process of writing. We can teach them to be more reflective about their writing so they know what type of help they need and how to request it. We can teach children to graciously accept suggestions from others and to anticipate that response will help their writing get better. We can teach them to respond to each other with respect and kindness and to use the language of writers, so that they learn to trust and value each other's feedback.

Instructional Benefits

- Authentic, positive, and constructive response creates energy and desire for students to revise their writing.

- Retelling ideas, with or without reading the text aloud, serves as oral rehearsal for writing that helps students remember and crystalize their intentions and revise in the moment as they talk.

- Talking about writing with partners and in small groups reinforces the idea that writers gather, borrow, and grow ideas from and with others.

- Students begin to take up the compliments we give and the strategies we teach in conferences, mimicking our language about writing as they respond to each other's writing.

- Being able to articulate a response to writing and even offer a suggestion for how to make it better helps children internalize that information for their own writing.

Social-emotional Benefits

- Response helps students understand the important role that encouragement and revision play in writing—and in life!

- The give-and-take of response teaches kids how to collaborate on projects, how to work through sticky situations and get to the other side when there is work to do together.

- A classroom filled with response teaches children the power of vulnerability—of being able to admit when they need help—and the power of advocating for themselves.

- When writers receive kind, supportive feedback over time, it builds confidence in themselves and in the writing process itself.

> "
> The offer of vulnerability and trust is precious, something we as teachers treasure—it helps make possible a relationship where both giver and receiver benefit. It's a big part of the reason we all wanted to become teachers in the first place.
>
> **THOMAS NEWKIRK** 2017, 64

Structures and Routines for Daily Response

Every day, we can offer our young writers response from us, their more experienced teachers, and also carve out time across the week for students to talk about their writing with peers in partnerships and small groups. Some of this talk will happen during independent writing time, and some of it will happen during the time set aside for sharing at the end of each day's workshop. Each context offers crucial feedback for growing writers and provides a variety of perspectives, tones, purposes, and strategies.

Writing Conferences

Writing Partnerships

Small Writing Groups

Share Time

Writing Conferences

During independent writing time, the teacher meets with individuals, partners, or small groups to name what students are doing well and to teach one tool or strategy they can use to move forward as writers. Writing conferences can happen at any point in the writing process, and in them we offer different kinds of responses, including simply listening. Most often, however, we serve as knowledgeable, experienced writing teachers with resources to share that will help students grow as writers. And because we are responding to one child's particular strengths and needs in conferences, our teaching tends to be deeper and more lasting than even the best minilesson.

A writing conference is a conversation between two people who both work at their writing. We should enter this space with curiosity, open to what is possible, and it matters how we position ourselves in this conversation. It matters whether we see the conference as a time to point out errors we find and tell students exactly what they need to fix, or embrace it as a chance to name students' strengths and give them tools to build on those strengths. One way of being in the conference depletes confidence and may cause kids to hate writing; the other gives them joy and energy to put their voices on the page, to revise, and to see themselves as capable writers.

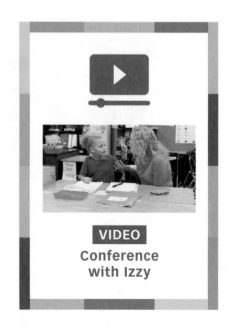

VIDEO
Conference with Izzy

How to Have a Writing Conference

1. Position yourself side by side with a student who is writing.

2. Ask an open-ended question:

   → "What are you working on in your writing today?"

   → "What are you thinking as you write today?"

   → "What are your plans for your writing today?"

3. Listen. Observe. Gather information. Make notes.

4. Name something the student is already doing well as a writer.

5. Decide on one point—a skill, strategy, or craft technique—to teach; one that will help not only on this particular piece but every time the student writes this kind of text.

6. Teach that one point using one or more of these tools:

   → Explain it.

   → Demonstrate it.

   → Refer to a mentor text (your writing, student writing, or published writing) that shows what you want to teach.

7. Check for understanding, and then remind the student that they can use this skill, strategy, or craft technique not only now but any time in the future.

8. End on a positive note. Tell the student you can't wait to read what they come up with next!

9. Document your teaching in writing.

Conferring at a Glance

Tips for Efficient and Effective Writing Conferences

Mind your timing

Every student needs regular response from the teacher, so learning how to pace your conferences is critical. Here are some metrics to work with that can help you get to each of your students on a regular basis:

- Meet for five to seven minutes per student.
- Aim for meeting with four to six students per day during independent writing.
- Confer with every student in your class at least once a week.
- Keep a weekly checklist to see at a glance whom you have conferred with.
- Confer with students who have writing challenges *no more* than twice a week. You don't want them to depend on you to get through the hard parts; rather, you want to teach them strategies they can use independently.

Document your conferences using some type of form

Each conference is part of an ongoing conversation, and each new response you give builds from the ones before it. Therefore, you need to record what students say they are doing, what they do well, and what you taught them so you can look back at this information before your next conference. Find a record-keeping format that works well for you (a checklist, a sticky note with the student's name on it, a blank notebook with a section for each child in your class).

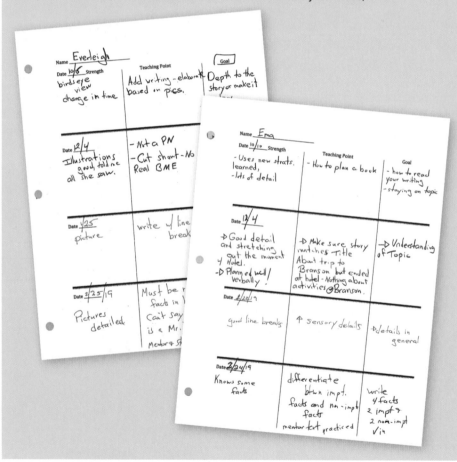

Use your writing notebook as you confer

Your stance in a writing conference is as one writer responding to another, so let your notebook do the talking. Rather than endlessly explaining what to do, turn to a place in your notebook and show the student how you tried three different endings to your story or how you planned your feature article in a web graphic organizer.

Give students a record of your teaching points

The cumulative effect of your teaching over time helps students' learning stick. To remind students of what you talked about and the strategies they tried, copy mini–anchor charts for kids to glue into their writing notebooks or keep in folders where they can write notes on their conferences.

> " Our first job in a conference, then, is to be a person, not just a teacher. It is to enjoy, to care, to respond. We cry, laugh, nod, and sigh. We let the writer know she has been heard.
>
> **LUCY CALKINS** 1986, 118

VIDEO
Teaching from Your Own Writing

Writing Conferences = Formative Assessment

Response is not only what we "say back" to children. It is a stance we take to our teaching and learning relationship with them. Everything we say and do and plan should be *in response* to the children sitting in front of us.

During conferences, our ongoing, in-the-moment assessment of students' writing and also what they *say* about their writing provide authentic data about how students are doing and what else they need to learn. We also assess as we confer with partners and small groups, observe kids as they work, and read student writing outside workshop time. We keep records of what we hear, see, and read, and as we reread our notes, we notice, perhaps, that many children would benefit from a reteach of today's lesson, or a reminder of a lesson from two months ago, or a lesson about a specific craft feature of the genre we are studying. This is formative assessment in a nutshell: we form our decisions about what to teach based precisely on what the children sitting in front of us *need* to continue writing.

Formative Assessment Form

Sample Conferring Forms

Keeping Notes on Writing Conferences

We find that busy teachers will document their writing conferences when they find a system that makes sense for them. No single note-taking format works for every teacher, so we offer these suggestions to help you think about how you might create such a system:

- Do you have space to make these notes?
  - → the student's name and date
  - → anecdotal notes about the student's choices (time, space, materials, topics, genres)
  - → writing strengths
  - → writing goals

- Is there a way to see progress across time in your notes?
- Is there room for multiple entries on a page?
- How will you keep notes together and transport them as you meet with children?
- How will you monitor trends across your students to guide small-group and whole-class instruction?

Avoid making assumptions about how to respond to students' writing based on their grade level or age. Assumptive teaching often leads to

- weekly (even monthly or yearly!) predetermined lesson plans
- adherence to rigid grade-level expectations and omission of a continuum of writing development
- persistence in a plan regardless of the needs of many students ("We have so much to get to!")
- wasteful minilessons that cover content and processes students may already know and be able to do.

take a bow!

These are our go-to books for learning how to confer with writers:

A Teacher's Guide to Writing Conferences and *How's It Going? A Practical Guide to Conferring with Student Writers*, by Carl Anderson.

Hidden Gems: Naming and Teaching from the Brilliance in Every Student's Writing, by Katherine Bomer.

"The Listening Eye: Reflections on the Writing Conference," by Donald Murray, in *The Essential Don Murray*.

Writing Partnerships

For most young people, no one is more exciting to write for than their peers. In writing partnerships, students share what they are working on and provide support and suggestions for making their writing better. Depending on the routines you establish, students might work with partners during independent writing time or during share time at the end of writing workshop—or both.

Inviting your students to *choose* partners they feel comfortable sharing with creates independence, responsibility, and engagement in the work of writing. However, depending on your management style and the social tenor of your classroom, you might choose partners or simply have students share with the person sitting next to them.

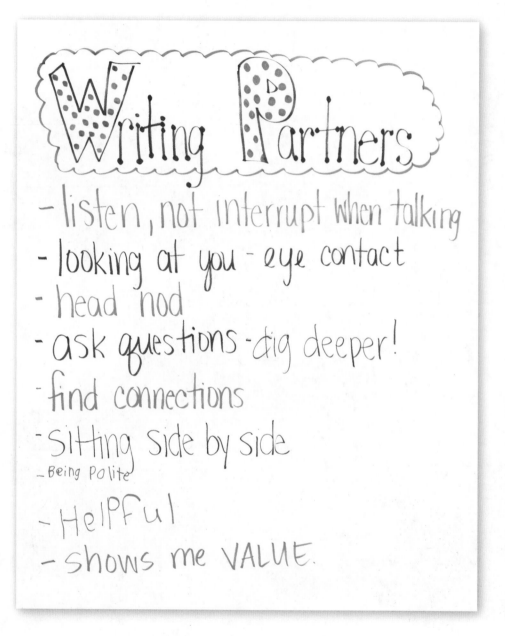

Students Working in a Writing Partnership

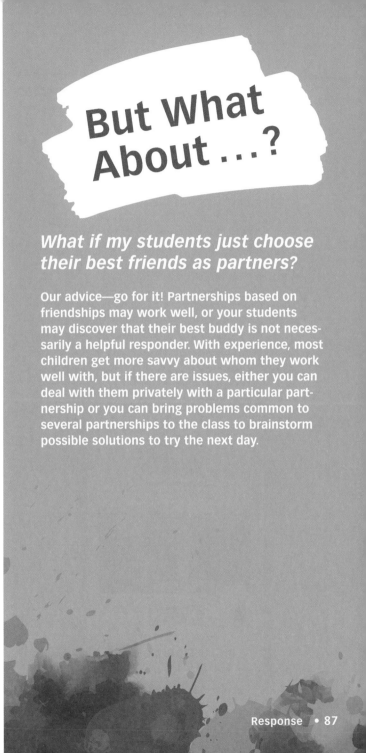

But What About ...?

What if my students just choose their best friends as partners?

Our advice—go for it! Partnerships based on friendships may work well, or your students may discover that their best buddy is not necessarily a helpful responder. With experience, most children get more savvy about whom they work well with, but if there are issues, either you can deal with them privately with a particular partnership or you can bring problems common to several partnerships to the class to brainstorm possible solutions to try the next day.

Once kids pair up, even the youngest writers can learn to respond helpfully to each other's writing *if* we take the time to teach them how to do it. Later we'll look at some specific teaching you can do to support peer response, but here are some early-in-the-year teaching points for successful writing partnerships just to get kids started:

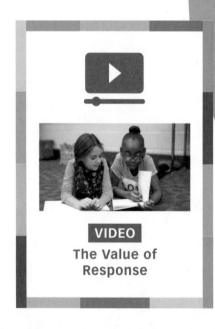

VIDEO
The Value of Response

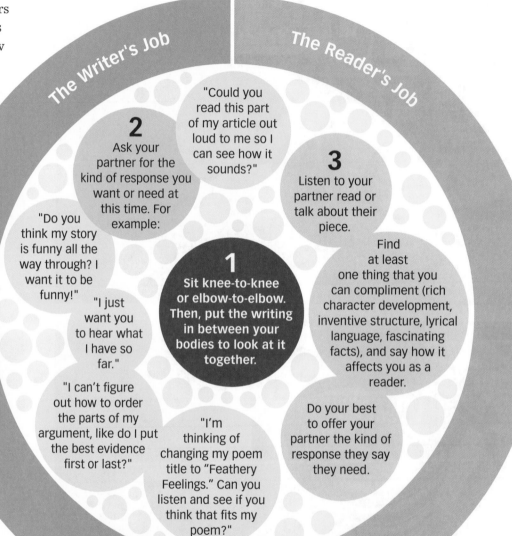

The Writer's Job

The Reader's Job

2
Ask your partner for the kind of response you want or need at this time. For example:

"Could you read this part of my article out loud to me so I can see how it sounds?"

3
Listen to your partner read or talk about their piece.

"Do you think my story is funny all the way through? I want it to be funny!"

"I just want you to hear what I have so far."

1
Sit knee-to-knee or elbow-to-elbow. Then, put the writing in between your bodies to look at it together.

Find at least one thing that you can compliment (rich character development, inventive structure, lyrical language, fascinating facts), and say how it affects you as a reader.

"I can't figure out how to order the parts of my argument, like do I put the best evidence first or last?"

"I'm thinking of changing my poem title to "Feathery Feelings." Can you listen and see if you think that fits my poem?"

Do your best to offer your partner the kind of response they say they need.

But What About...?

How often do partnerships and groups need to be changed?

If your partnerships and small groups are giving each other kind, constructive feedback, why mess that up? You don't necessarily need to change them, but be sure you consistently assess partnerships and groups so you know if members are working well together. If they're not, the difficulties they face can become rich sites for instruction. Sit beside the groups, observe, and then offer strategies to help them. You might also ask your students periodically if they want new partners or groups. Sometimes switching them up brings the energy of new perspectives to the work of writers.

Small Writing Groups

For older students (grades three and above), another structure for response is the small writing group—four to five students who share what they are working on and talk about places in the process that feel tricky or difficult. A small group widens the pool of response and learning for everyone, as students often see things differently. Writers who receive response from a group have more perspectives to consider and, as a result, more decisions to make.

Groups can be formed by simply joining two partnerships, but by midyear, if your students have been writing and sharing every day, they will know each other fairly well as writers. They will know, for instance, that they need to practically beg Tonya to read her work out loud, but once she does, she beams from everyone's enthusiastic response. Or that Jae, who is super-confident about his hysterically funny writing, just wants someone to edit his spelling so he can get better at it.

When students know each other as writers, you might invite them to think about who would be great to work with in a group—and why. Have them write letters to you explaining why they are eager to work with three or four specific writers in the class. Then, study the letters, make a flowchart of possible groupings, and try to give each student at least one requested group member. Either of these grouping options saves kids from possible social distress and hurt feelings.

Share Time

Students need regular opportunities to share their thinking about what they are writing, their plans for what they will do next, what they are struggling with or confused about, or some bit of the writing itself. Knowing this, we set aside five to seven minutes of the workshop for share time. Most often, we bring the class together to listen to a few children share what they are working on. Then, the audience offers positive response, questions, and suggestions to the writers.

From experience, we know that it's easy to let the time for sharing get away from us. We get so caught up in all the activity of writing time that we find ourselves with just three minutes left to get all thirty kids to their computer class! The quandary is real, but we have to work hard not to let this daily structure disappear. Share time is a powerful, flexible teaching and learning tool we can use in different ways depending on our needs. The key is that it happens daily, children's writing is the focus, and response is the purpose. Share time

- usually happens at the end of each writing session, though sometimes we might "stop the presses" in the middle of writing time to spotlight a strategy someone used or a breakthrough someone had

- can happen occasionally at the beginning of the workshop, and the topic for the minilesson comes from reflecting on what you discover from sharing

- can be one to three students sharing in front of the whole class in the meeting area, perhaps sitting on a "share chair" or "author's chair"

- can be every student reading a small part of their work out loud, possibly going around a circle in the meeting area

VIDEO

A Student Teaches the Class

can be partnerships or small groups meeting to share on their own. (This might be a regularly scheduled activity, perhaps twice a week during share time, or it might happen according to writers' needs during independent writing time.)

Partnerships and small groups generally set their own agendas for sharing, but when the whole class is gathered, you'll want to think about both *who* will share and *what* they will share. Remember this is an additional teaching opportunity, so be intentional about how you use it. You can learn a lot from a "survey the room" type of share, but if you want every voice to be heard, students will need a specific, narrow focus for their sharing (or else it will go on too long). If you select just a few students to share, they can explore their work more deeply, especially if you ask them to reflect on their work through some lens. The chart on the right depicts examples of frames for both kinds of sharing, but the possibilities are really limitless.

The more students articulate the journey of writing and hear others do the same, the more they begin to internalize the process and understand what works and doesn't work for each of them. When they share every day, your students learn to listen well, to give each other ideas and teach each other strategies, and to celebrate each other's work.

If most students are sharing . . .

Share a favorite sentence from your writing in your best read-aloud voice.

Share just the topic you are writing about, so we can see the richness of your ideas.

In one sentence, tell us something you've recently learned from another writer in the room.

Read the working title of your piece so we can wonder what it might be about.

Name the part of the writing process you find most challenging, and explain why.

If just two or three students are sharing . . .

Share before-and-after versions of some sentence you revised today, and explain your decision.

Tell us about a place where you had problems but figured out what to do. How did you solve them?

Share a favorite paragraph you wrote today, and tell us why you like it.

Teach us what you learned in a conference (or partnership) today.

Show us something you did in your writing that you learned from a mentor text.

But What About...?

What about students who don't want to share with the whole class?

Students who haven't shared their writing much may be hesitant or fear going public with it. You can nurture their willingness to share and watch their courage evolve over time by providing safety nets like these:

- reading only one sentence with a friend
- passing on sharing for a while, until they see how much fun it is to have an audience
- sharing a drawing instead of their writing
- talking about what they've written rather than reading it.

Thinking About Beginning Writers

Because they need to talk *as* they write, and because they write fewer words, our youngest writers share practically every mark they make on paper every day! But whole-class sharing is still valuable because it does so much teaching work. You might need to sit next to children as they share and guide them to talk about their process. Ask them questions about how they did things and where they got their ideas. If they're not yet able to read their writing back, have them tell the class about it and respond just as you would if they had read the print.

Teaching Students About the Give-and-Take of Response

Once you have the structures and routines for daily response established, there is so much for students to learn about how to do this work well together. As groups and partnerships are discussing their writing, you can first observe and then teach something that will lift the level of the responsive talk you see and hear. In addition to conferring, you can also support students with minilessons that help them learn about the give-and-take of response.

Making Feedback More Specific

What does a meaningful conversation—writer to writer—*sound* like? We can teach students that when two "insiders" get together to talk, the conversation should be both respectful and resourceful. Respect comes from the fact that they both understand the challenging work of writing, and the conversation is resourceful when they are specific in the feedback they offer. Stopping at "I love it!" or "Add more details" does not give a writer a vision for what they can do, or need to do more of, in the future. Instead, students need to watch and listen for what sparks their partner's interest and excitement as they talk about their writing, and then name it specifically.

We can also teach students that *how* they say things matters and that the tone of their feedback should always be generous and supportive. For example, have them consider how they respond when a writer's meaning is unclear. As a reader they might say, "I want to understand this part better" or "I was a bit confused right here. Can you tell me what you are thinking or want to say?" In contrast, if they just come out and say, "This essay doesn't make sense," they change the writer-to-writer tone of the

Make feedback that's general . . .	. . . much more specific.
Wow! You really know how to argue!	I noticed you made the point of your argument so vivid when you included this story about your little brother who lived with this illness. No wonder you are so passionate about it!
You're so creative! You're a good story writer.	The way you use dialogue makes your characters sound like real people. The mom *sounds* just like my mom!
It sounds kind of a little boring, to be honest.	You could study the voice in some sports columns online or in the newspaper to weave in more of that sports-caster tone you have in the first few sentences.

conference and could cause their partner to lose confidence. Instead, their response should help their partner begin to internalize "the reader" and become aware when their exciting story or the point of their argument is or is not as clear as it might be.

Responding in Different Ways

As we said, when students don't have a lot of experience talking as writers, they tend to be too general in the give-and-take of response. "Do you like it?" a writer will ask. "Yes, it's great!" they hear in response. To help them become more resourceful and specific, teach students that while their first job is to be a cheerleader for each other's writing, there are different types of specific response they can give and receive.

Respond as a *reader.*

Sometimes writers need someone to . . .	What it sounds like
. . . simply love the way they write, or the story they tell, or agree with their argument for more time to play in the school day.	"I *love* this poem."
	"This reminds me of the ending of a fairy tale."
Writers also need someone to help them understand what sense the text is and isn't making.	"The language here sounds almost like you are giving a sermon! Maybe it's a little too preachy?"
	"I'm confused in this part—is this happening in the past or right now?"

Respond as a *collaborator.*

Sometimes writers need someone to . . .	What it sounds like
. . . help them dream, problem solve, or imagine new possibilities.	"What if you tried moving this part up to the beginning?"
	"You could just leave this whole section out."
	"What if you interviewed someone who was there to get a quote for this part?"

Respond as a *listener.*

Sometimes writers need someone to . . .

. . . talk something through with—an idea, a struggle, a decision that needs to be made.

What it sounds like

"What I hear you saying is that you don't think the ending is working."

"Do you think it would help to put this away for a while and come back to it after some rest?"

Respond as a *critic.*

Sometimes writers need someone to . . .

. . . name what's not working.

What it sounds like

"It's clear you did a lot of research about volcanoes, but it's not that interesting because there are too many facts. Could you maybe add someone's story or personal connection?"

"The honest truth? Some people might think referring to her as 'Shorty' is not funny. It could be seen as bullying."

Respond as a *teacher.*

Sometimes writers need someone to . . .

. . . show them how to do something.

What it sounds like

"Let's look at how Jason Reynolds tags his dialogue."

"Let me show you the difference between telling and showing."

"You could take this one line and write a whole page off it. See where the thinking takes you."

Respond as an *editor.*

Sometimes writers need someone to . . .

. . . help them check their proofreading for accuracy.

What it sounds like

"In this sentence, you need a comma after the word *sentence* because it's like a little introductory phrase."

"I think it should be *principle* instead of *principal.*"

"You need a heading here to make it match the other sections."

In a single working session, a good partner moves in and out of these different response styles based on what the writer needs and where the conversation goes. For the responder, the point is *not* to settle on one type of response or another but to follow the writer's lead.

There are several ways you can teach students about these different kinds of responses. Rather than assigning the different response types as *roles* to play, it is much better to catch students doing them naturally as they talk with each other about their writing, and then name what *purpose* that kind of response has. For example, suppose you hear a student say to their partner, "I have a great idea! Maybe all the power goes out, and the kids, cats, and dog are stranded in the closet under the stairs!" You can give feedback on what you overheard, saying, "You're really helping your partner imagine new possibilities. Great writing partners inspire each other with ideas, just like that!" Notice that the emphasis is on naming the specific purpose of the feedback, which in this case is a kind of collaboration on ideas. Later, during share time, you might ask these partners to talk about how they supported each other, and then name the purpose of the feedback for the whole class. From this work over time, you can create an ongoing anchor chart of constructive ways writers can respond to each other.

Another way to teach students about different kinds of response is to have partnerships or small groups work together in a "fishbowl" with the rest of the class watching and taking notes on what they hear and see. From this, you can generalize about feedback that is more and less helpful for writers and add to your anchor chart. Students also benefit from hearing examples of exact language that serve different feedback purposes, so you might record these on the chart as well.

Different Kinds of Responses

VIDEO

Teaching into Small-Group Work

> " Audience matters. Through the audience's immediate response—body language, facial expression, clarifying information, telling back what they heard, and asking questions—the teller (writer) finds out that what is interesting to him can be interesting to others. They also learn how the listeners (readers) heard their story and begin to learn that they have to include certain information if they want their readers to understand.

MARTHA HORNE AND MARY ELLEN GIACOBBE 2007,17

Thinking About Beginning Writers

While learning to be more intentional about the give-and-take of response is sophisticated work, it's not out of reach for beginning writers. Many young children love to show each other how to do things, and you can capitalize on that energy as you support their partnerships. The key is to keep the teaching developmentally appropriate and focused on their actual needs. This means, of course, that a lot of their talk might be about their drawings. Illustrators use the same process writers use to plan, draft, revise, and edit a picture, so students can talk about this process in all the same ways.

Asking for Specific Help as a Writer

The more students learn about different kinds of responses, the better they will be able to advocate for their own needs as writers—but don't leave this learning to chance. Teach students how to articulate a specific need and then how to ask for help to address it. Almost always, the key is to frame the request so their partner says or does something in response that will help them. For example, asking, "Does it make sense?" and having their partner say, "Yes!" is not specific enough to be useful. Hearing different ways to ask for help gives writers the vision and the language for what to ask for, so chart possibilities whenever you talk about this with students.

Framing the kind of response you need so your partner will say a lot back is a first step, but to really advocate for themselves, writers also need to ask for more information when they need it. Teach your students how to dig deeper with questions like these:

> *Can you say more about that?*
>
> *When you said _____, what did you mean exactly?*
>
> *Can you point to a specific place in my piece that matches what you're saying?*
>
> *Let me say back what I hear you saying. Correct me if I'm wrong, or let me know if there are other things you want to add.*

Getting What You Need as a Writer

If you need this as a writer . . .	ask your partner or group . . .
You want a general impression of the impact of your writing.	"Can you read this and tell me what you think?"
You're not sure whether you're getting to the heart of what you're writing.	"Will you read this and then say back to me what you think I'm really trying to say?"
You question whether the organization of your writing is logical to a reader.	"Does the way I've chunked my information make sense to you?" Or "Can you follow the plot?"
You have no idea how to end your piece so it feels satisfying to the reader.	"Will you read this and then help me think of ways I could end it?"
You need to cut, so you want to know which parts of the writing seem most and least interesting to a reader.	"In your opinion, which parts of this could you do without as a reader?"
You're worried that the tone of your writing might be too harsh.	"Will you read this with a high-lighter in hand and mark any places where you think my words might sound too angry?"
You're not sure if your writing has "gaps" in it—things that don't add up for the reader.	"Please read this, and then let's talk about any questions it raises for you."

What Do Writers *Do* with Response?

Finally, we also need to show our students what to do with the response they ask for and receive. It can be difficult for writers (of any age) to open themselves to feedback. Some become defensive, some feel embarrassed that they perhaps did something wrong, and still others worry that accepting their partners' suggestions for revision means that the idea is no longer their own.

We can help students see that writers often learn new things from others who read their work and they know the writing will be even better with feedback. On the right are some steps to share with students that show them how to make use of feedback in a safe and collaborative writing workshop:

When you see that writers have really used feedback to make their writing better, have them share this with the class. They can show the before and after of the writing and talk about the decisions they made based on their partners' feedback. In no time at all, students will see the value of response and truly look forward to meeting with their partners or small groups.

What to Do with Response

Step 1	Step 2	Step 3
Thank your partners for their careful reading or listening and for offering advice and ideas to make your writing better.	If possible, take notes on what your partners say on sticky notes and place them in the spot you need to revise. Or you could just keep notes in your writing notebook to refer to later.	Look over all the feedback you received to see if it makes sense for what you want your writing to look and sound like. You are the author, and it's up to you to decide whether you want to try your friends' ideas or not.

Step 4	Step 5	Step 6
For editing suggestions (grammar, spelling, and punctuation), decide if you think your partners' advice is correct or not. You may disagree, and if you do, it might be helpful to talk the issue through with them, or even get a second or third opinion. But if your partners are correct, just be grateful they caught the mistake!	Take action. Revise or edit your writing based on your decisions.	If the response you received leads you somewhere wonderful in your writing, don't keep it to yourself. Let your partners know how helpful they were.

> " It is a matter of faith, faith that my students have something to say and a language in which to say it.
>
> **DONALD MURRAY** 2009, 153

TIME, CHOICE, **AND** RESPONSE **IN ACTION**

Response

Abigail's poem was published alongside the photograph that inspired it and placed in her teacher's classroom library, becoming a powerful social studies resource now and for years to come.

Choice

Like all poets, Abigail is deeply influenced by books, photographs, and art. Here she chose to write about a Holocaust photograph where people were alone—not physically, but in their minds, wondering how anyone could be so evil.

Time

Because poems have few words, even a tiny revision can change rhythm, emphasis, and meaning. Abigail put her poem draft away for a few days, then reread it and made new line breaks and stanzas, additions and deletions. Poets know that it takes time to think and re-see to find the best words and form.

Demo

in age of black/and white,

and war.

as they wait Cold /sick and alone

with the sound of /screams/and suffring

fill the //// air
       Dark
the people so ~~tring~~/there bones
              tired disire there
                   the people
can be seen hunger to stop

even children so new to this world

can leave/just as fast

trains drop these people off

and at Gun point

walk to the end if there suffring.

---

in a age of black and white
war.

as they wait Cold
sick
and alone

with sounds of suffring and pain
drown out the sound of breathing

people who want nothing more than
a happy dream

even Children so new takes
deaths hand with joy

a train drops them off

and at gun point

walk to the end

of suffring.

A.H

Extending Response Beyond the Walls of the Classroom

Publication

Inside the word *publication* is the word *public*, as in seen or heard and appreciated by people outside the classroom. When we publish their writing, children learn that there are true purposes and rewards to writing that practice inside the classroom cannot replicate sufficiently. In addition to publishing the more traditional genres like stories, poems, or feature articles, we can also find other forms that help students' writing work go public: a note written to the principal, custodian, or another teacher; labels on objects and places around the school; posters and banners in the hallway; playbills for the school musical; letters to the city council or newspaper; announcements read over the public address system; speeches made on the Capitol steps. Here are some more ideas for going public with writing:

- Display writing on classroom walls or in the school hallways, cafeteria, teachers' lounge, or child and adult restrooms so that school spaces are literally dripping with every child's art and writing.

A Sign Displayed by the Recess Doors

Books by Students Displayed in the Classroom Library

- Design a class magazine or newsletter.

- Record students reading their writing out loud, make QR codes to attach to the writing, and publish the recordings online.

- Place writing in the class library so students can read each other's work.

- Invite the school librarian to create bar codes for student works that can be checked out along with regular library books.

- Host a weekly "open mic" session over the PA system during lunch.

- Ask a local public library or coffee shop for permission to display student writing for a specific length of time.

- Record podcasts of students reading and talking about their work.

- Publish on online platforms such as Vimeo, Animoto, and Powtoon.

- With permission, celebrate students in online spaces: tweet out beautiful sentences and lines of poetry they've written; share on the school or class website or blog.

When their work goes public, adult writers receive everything from rave reviews to curmudgeonly critiques. Thankfully, children receive almost exclusively positive response to their finished writing, and they love receiving notes and letters from readers. We know that they internalize this kind of response, using it to inform their future writing projects.

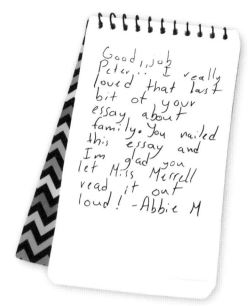

Response accumulates over the year in these mini-notebooks.

Celebrations

We can elevate students' finished writing even more by attaching celebrations to our publishing. Reading to an audience of students from other classrooms, or family members, or strangers at a coffee shop, gives kids the instant gratification of laughter, tears, sighs, and applause. This real and enthusiastic response from loving humans tends to create little "writing enthusiasts," who say, "When can we write again!?"

While clapping and cheering goes a long way toward making a celebration memorable, you might also build in time for the audience to ask your students questions about the content or process of their writing. When children respond to questions from interested readers, they find ways to articulate their thinking. This helps them internalize the process and affects how they think about the writing task the next time they sit down to compose.

Here are a few ideas for planning writing celebrations:

- Invite another class or two to listen to your students' writing.

- Invite families and guests to the classroom or a borrowed space (the library, art room, or music room) to hear students read their work out loud.

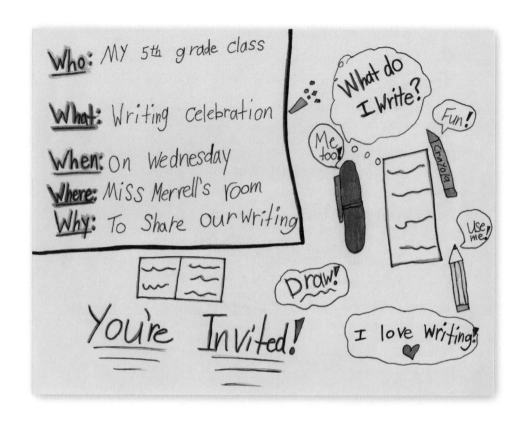

- Hang writing on walls or place it around the room on tables and invite guests to walk around and read and enjoy the pieces. Make note cards or sticky notes and pens available for guests to write positive comments and connections.

- Plan a school-wide celebration, for instance, a night to celebrate the poetry the whole school has been writing for three or four weeks, or a weeklong celebration of the writing happening at each grade level.

Supporting Appreciative Response

Celebrate the Writing Process

You can send a message about the value of process by placing notebook entries or parts of drafts alongside an attractive, persuasive display that explains how writing looks much like a house or apartment building as it is being constructed. There are scaffolds holding it up; there are tools lying around; and it might be difficult to imagine what it will look like in the end, but how cool is it to see the skeleton of the building! Here are some other ideas for celebrating the writing process:

- Ask students to find their favorite notebook entry. Copy and hang these entries in the hallway, with an invitation for people to read and notice the thinking students are doing.

- When displaying published pieces of writing in the hallway, online, or during writing celebrations, include drafts with revisions alongside the final draft of writing.

- Ask students to write a short reflection about their process and share it with guests along with the finished writing. In their reflection, students might answer questions like these:

  → What did you learn?

  → What revisions did you try?

  → What partner responses helped you revise?

  → What else might you do if you had another week or more to work on this piece?

A hallway bulletin board showcases students' notebook entries.

Writing Workshop and Multilingual Students

Every person learns language by first hearing it whispered, sung, shouted, and repeated all around them, and then *using* it to get what they want and need, to ask questions, to tell secrets. As children grow, they build oral fluency, including the names of important people and things and the concepts of language and syntax, that they can use as stepping-stones into written literacy in school.

The same process is true for children learning English as another language. We must embrace students' more familiar oral and written languages as allies and celebrate ways they actually make English refreshingly new and poetic. In the writing workshop, daily *talk* about writing is important rehearsal as kids access the words they need to represent their ideas. Talk builds language skills and confidence, so we must offer multiple routines for students to talk with us and with writing partners. Here are ways to enhance response for multilingual students:

- Confer with students accompanied by a language broker (someone in the room who speaks both languages and knows a bit more English), who can help them find words.

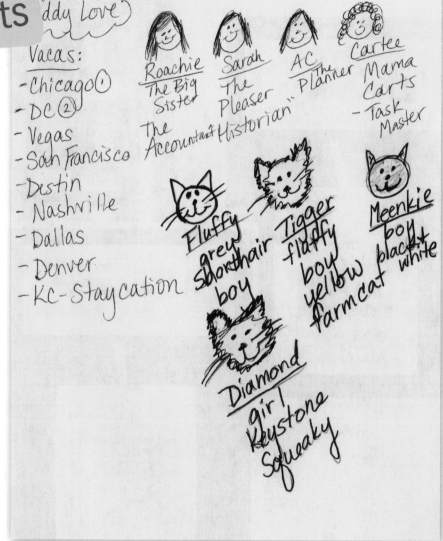

A teacher makes sketches to use in writing conferences.

- Use visuals and sketches to help you say what you mean in minilessons and writing conferences.

- Encourage students to choose partners who can act as language brokers. If you do not have multiple speakers of a certain language, encourage your students to choose a partner who will give plenty of wait time and silence, read the writing with appreciative eyes, and be able to help their friend feel comfortable to take risks and make mistakes.

- Encourage students to think of a specific person they are writing for. Often, when kids can picture their grandmother reading their memoir or their cousin learning some cool moves from their video game manual, they will bring their full linguistic competence, in their home language and/or in English, to help the piece be the best it can be.

- Invite students to publish and read pieces that contain their home language at celebrations.

- Ask for help translating any verbal or written comments to the students' writing so they get the full joy and benefits of positive response.

Time, Choice, and Response
Across a School Year

The end

When you document and reflect on your students' writing from the beginning of the year to the end, you can actually see their attitudes and abilities grow and change over time. To this end, we recommend you keep your students' writing work in portfolios or hanging files so that together you can lay early work beside end-of-year work to reread and note how everything, from handwriting and spelling, to paragraphing, to storytelling, picture book illustrating, journalistic reporting, speechwriting, and poetry making, has matured and changed. Handing the portfolios to their authors to reflect on their own growth (alone or with partners) across time can be quite energizing and rewarding for your student writers.

We have found it helpful to think of growth in writing across a school year as a continuum of progress in understandings, skills, identities, and responsibilities, rather than a discrete set of "grade-level" standards to check off. The next few pages describe attitudes and behaviors around writing that teachers and students tend to demonstrate early in the year and later in the year in writing workshop. Though these markers do not usually appear on rubrics or in test scores, they contribute greatly to helping students improve those rubric scores, and more importantly, they describe authentic attributes that students need to become accomplished writers for life.

Reflecting on Work over Time

What You Will Likely See Early in the Year

- Students using pictures as writing. Drawing *is* writing for the youngest students and sometimes even for many older students who think and communicate visually, or who are not yet comfortable, for a variety of reasons, with writing.

- Students making their thoughts visible in pictures, words, lists, charts, webs, and diagrams.

A primary student uses spelling approximations to write nonfiction.

- Approximations of spelling, punctuation, visual representations, and text forms.

- Writing notebooks (grades three and up) with lists of possible topics, tryouts of different kinds of writing, writing to think, sketches, and plans for writing.

My feelings

In my feelings. I feel greatness and
weakness. Wizdom and sadness.

Excitement and sorrow. Confutation

And energy. So, when you put that all

Together that makes me.

Approximation supports
an intermediate student
learning to write poetry
and use a keyboard.

Early in the Year

If teachers are . . .	Then students are . . .
Building a writing community: accepting the particular gifts students bring with them, and not correcting and grading.	Discovering themselves as writers or reflecting on their histories as writers.
Creating a safe, comfortable, and productive space for students to practice writing and to share their writing.	Becoming risk-takers and learning to find ideas for writing by paying attention to their hearts, minds, and lives.
Establishing routines, rituals, and procedures: how to gather in the minilesson area; how to leave the minilesson and find writing spots; how and where to get materials; when and where to meet with writing partners.	Growing independence for getting tools and materials when needed, choosing writing spots where powerful writing work can happen, and learning how to work through social-emotional difficulties with writing partners.
Demonstrating that writers have choice in what to write about by showing the different ideas, topics, people, and places that they can write from.	Developing trust that their teachers will accept and support their topic choices, which results in increasing enthusiasm and focus on writing, for longer amounts of time.
Accepting without critique or judgment the topics young people love to write about.	
Getting to know students as writers: researching, observing, listening, assessing, and giving appreciative response to kids in writing conferences.	Getting to know each other as writers by sharing and responding positively to bits of writing, as well as through the processes of writing every day.
Teaching from their own writing process by using portions of writing from their notebooks and drafts.	Getting to know their teachers as writers and learning from the strategies they share for working through tricky parts.
Researching and building theories of writers' identities, strengths, and areas to grow.	Developing language for writing from the teacher's minilessons and conferences, from study of mentor texts, and from peers.
Collecting information that will inform instruction.	

> "What [students] require is a teacher who will respect and respond... not for what they have produced, but for what they will produce, if they are given an opportunity to see writing as a process, not a product.
>
> DONALD MURRAY 2009, 5

What You Will Likely See as the Year Progresses

- More creative and controlled writing, because students are blossoming as they practice writing every day.

- More purposeful and genuinely supportive student-led writing partnerships and small groups.

- Increased energy and focus for sitting and writing, for longer periods of time.

- Higher levels of confidence and self-efficacy in students, which come from experience. Everyone in this community writes to the best of their ability.

- Students writing outside the writing workshop, for instance, choosing to write during "free time;" writing at home or on holidays, during recess, or on the school bus; or purchasing their own writing notebooks.

- Students creating independent writing projects, such as collaborative pieces, blogs, plots for video games, picture books for younger students, YouTube videos, podcasts, or plays to perform for the class.

Later in the Year

If teachers are . . .	Then students are . . .
Giving more explicit writing instruction (in conferences and mini-lessons) in response to student needs.	Asking more specific questions about composition and skills (in conferences and partnerships) as they begin to take ownership of their writing process.
Giving less explicit instruction regarding management and logistics.	Acting more independently as writers and self-directed learners and managing their writing time, space, and materials.
Giving most of the responsibility to students for managing the process and pacing of writing.	Relying on their own decision making about when they need to elaborate the middle section of their story, or when it's time to move from their writers' notebooks to type a draft on the computer.
	Deciding they prefer to talk before writing, or who might be the best partner to help push them toward a deadline.
	Determining how long to work on different parts of the process and when they are finished.
Deepening the level of response to student writing as students gain more control of the composing process.	Articulating their own writing processes, knowing what works best for them, and naming what gets in the way.
	Using writing language and genre knowledge with increasing confidence, recognizing places in their writing that can be elaborated and revised, and making personal goals for growth.
Deepening the sophistication of partner work through teaching and coaching.	Giving more detailed, specific responses to their peers.
	Taking the feedback of their peers seriously and making revisions to their writing based on that feedback.

"I'm the Kind of Writer Who . . ."

Perhaps the most important outcome of supporting students with time, choice, and response across the school year is that they develop such strong identities as writers. These confident identities are so clear in this video where Jackson and Tate, the two writers you met at the very start of this book, talk about their work.

Watching these fourth graders talk about their creation of over 160 illustrated chapter books, we feel we are listening to a couple of famous graphic novelists, for the language they use and the processes they describe are exactly like what seasoned writers say and do; for example, they say they get their ideas "from everyday things that happen" and "off of books in the classroom, just twisting the title a little bit." Tate says he likes "the feeling of getting what you're imagining off your mind, pencil to paper." We could not have said it better.

What we love most as we watch these authors is the way they seem to adore each other's writing. Tate begins smiling before Jackson even starts reading book #48 because he knows this book well. He knows exactly when the character "Jackson the Cow" poops "SPLAT!" on a floor at Walmart, and he is in giggles about it. He nods when his namesake and the central character from his own books, "T-Rex Tate," makes an

appearance to save the day. And Jackson clearly cracks up over Tate's expressive reading of the teeny chapter book "Forest Fire," which, Tate says, is not his "best," but it's his favorite. They can imperceptibly mouth the words of each other's books because they have been involved in the process of writing them together for so long and they have read them again and again, the way you would reread any favorite book when you were a child. They have so much influence on each other as writing partners that sometimes they will write the same book, just "from different perspectives," as Jackson puts it.

Jackson and Tate are talking about a series of books they have each been writing and illustrating for more than a year, since the beginning of third grade. This is a long time in a young person's life to sustain any project. Presumably, they will tire of these stories, but we have no doubt they will be on to new writing projects moments later. They work on their books constantly, during freewrite times in class and even during indoor recesses. They decide every single thing about their projects: when and with whom to write; what form to use (graphic fictional texts); what materials to use (pencil, markers, and colored pencils), and even the size and shape of some of the books. As a way to reuse and recycle almost a thousand plastic sleeves from Jackson's old game trading cards, for example, Tate invented a brand-new form of a teeny-tiny illustrated chapter book to house in all those sleeves.

No scripted writing assignment could result in such inventiveness, such intrinsic joy, and, we would argue, such skilled writing voice and craft. Only the edifice of writing workshop and the essential "bigs" that exist in their wonderful classrooms help their writing soar. Only choice could birth these quirky pieces of literature. Only time could produce over 160 different books. And only response could keep the motor running—from writing in their intense partnership to reading aloud to fan friends (and admiring teachers and coaches) who beg for more stories, feeding into the responsibility they feel not to let their audience down.

We wish this same joy and purpose for writing for each and every child in the world.

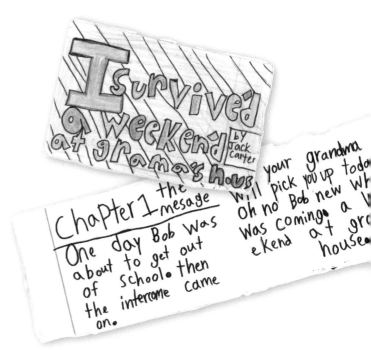

VIDEO
Jackson and Tate Talk About Coauthoring a Series

The Fox and the Frog
written by Kenneth

Once upon a time there were two neighbors. Their names were Fox and Frog. They lived near a pond. Frog was kind and friendly. Not like Fox, he was mean.

One day frog woke up with a headache. He called Fox to see if he could take care of him. Fox said, "No". Later that day Frog got better. Then Fox called to see if frog wanted to go to the park. Frog said, "no." Through his window he saw fox. He had a bag. Frog thought Fox was up to no good. The next day when frog woke up his phone started to ring. It was fox again. Fox was seeing if Frog wanted to go to the zoo. Frog said "no". Later that day when Frog was eating soup, he heard the phone he ignored it though.

Moral- Be kind to other people and they will be kind to you.

References

Anderson, Carl. 2000. *How's It Going? A Practical Guide to Conferring with Student Writers*. Portsmouth, NH: Heinemann.

———. 2018. *A Teacher's Guide to Writing Conferences*. Portsmouth, NH: Heinemann.

Bomer, Katherine. 2010. *Hidden Gems: Naming and Teaching from the Brilliance in Every Student's Writing*. Portsmouth, NH: Heinemann.

———. 2015. *The Journey Is Everything: Teaching Essays That Students Want to Write for People Who Want to Read Them*. Portsmouth, NH: Heinemann.

Bomer, Randy. 1995. *Time for Meaning: Crafting Literate Lives in Middle and High School*. Portsmouth, NH: Heinemann.

———. 2011. *Building Adolescent Literacy in Today's English Classrooms*. Portsmouth, NH: Heinemann.

Calkins, Lucy. 1986. *The Art of Teaching Writing*. 1st ed. Portsmouth, NH: Heinemann.

———. 1991. *Living Between the Lines*. Portsmouth, NH: Heinemann.

———. 1994. *The Art of Teaching Writing*. 2nd ed. Portsmouth, NH: Heinemann.

Fletcher, Ralph. 2003. *A Writer's Notebook: Unlocking the Writer Within You*. Reissue ed. New York: HarperCollins.

——— (@FletcherRalph). 2018. "The reading/writing workshop is an impressive machine with all sorts of conveyors, pulleys, bells & whistles. What fuel makes it work so well? Student choice. Remove that and the big apparatus quickly grinds to a halt. #JoyWrite #Greenbeltwriting." Twitter, October 23, 10:40 a.m. https://twitter.com/FletcherRalph/status/1054744275274084352.

Fox, Mem. 1993. *Radical Reflections: Passionate Opinions on Teaching, Learning, and Living*. New York: Harcourt.

Glover, Matt. 2020. *Craft and Process Studies*. Portsmouth, NH: Heinemann.

Graves, Donald H. 1983a. "The Growth and Development of First-Grade Writers." In *Learning to Write: First Language / Second Language*, edited by Aviva Freedman, Ian Pringle, and Janice Yalden, 54–66. London: Routledge.

———. 1983b. *Writing: Teachers and Children at Work*. Portsmouth, NH: Heinemann.

———. 1994. *A Fresh Look at Writing*. Portsmouth, NH: Heinemann.

———. 2013. Newkirk, Thomas, and Penny Kittle, eds. *Children Want to Write: Donald Graves and the Revolution in Children's Writing*. Portsmouth, NH: Heinemann.

Heard, Georgia. 2016. *HeartMaps: Helping Students Create and Craft Authentic Writing*. Portsmouth, NH: Heinemann.

Horne, Martha, and Mary Ellen Giacobbe. 2007. *Talking, Drawing, Writing: Lessons for Our Youngest Writers*. Portland, ME: Stenhouse.

Ladson-Billings, Gloria. 1995. "'But That's Just Good Teaching!' The Case for Culturally Relevant Pedagogy." *Theory into Practice* 34(3): 159–65.

Laman, Tasha Tropp. 2013. *From Ideas to Words: Writing Strategies for English Language Learners*. Portsmouth, NH: Heinemann.

Murray, Donald. 2009. Miller, Lisa, and Thomas Newkirk, eds. *The Essential Don Murray: Lessons from America's Greatest Writing Teacher*. Portsmouth, NH: Heinemann.

Newkirk, Thomas. 1989. *To Compose: Teaching Writing in High School and College*. Portsmouth, NH: Heinemann.

———. 2017. *Embarrassment and the Emotional Underlife of Learning*. Portsmouth, NH: Heinemann.

Palmer, Deborah K., and Ramón Antonio Martínez. 2016. "Developing Biliteracy: What Do Teachers *Really* Need to Know About Language?" *Language Arts* 93(5): 379–85.

Ray, Katie Wood. 2001. *The Writing Workshop: Working Through the Hard Parts (and They're All Hard Parts)*. Urbana, IL: National Council of Teachers of English.

———. 2006. *Study Driven: A Framework for Planning Units of Study in the Writing Workshop*. Portsmouth, NH: Heinemann.

Ray, Katie Wood, and Lisa Cleaveland. 2018. *A Teacher's Guide to Getting Started with Beginning Writers*. Portsmouth, NH: Heinemann.

Rowling, J. K. n.d. "J. K. Rowling > Quotes > Quotable Quote." Goodreads. Accessed June 25, 2019. www.goodreads.com/quotes/163742-be-ruthless-about-protecting-writing-days-i-e-do-not-cave.

Souto-Manning, Mariana, and Jessica Martell. 2016. *Reading, Writing, and Talk: Inclusive Teaching Strategies for Diverse Learners, K–2*. New York: Teachers College Press.

VanDerwater, Amy Ludwig. *Sharing Our Notebooks* (blog). http://www.sharingournotebooks.amylv.com.